preface

In my experience there is little science in assigning journalists to cover news stories. At BBC News I used to suggest that when you had dispatched sufficient reporters and production crews to cover a major story at home or overseas it was best to reflect for a while and then double the numbers to cope with the unexpected.

In past years the most time-consuming debate was not over the numbers of staff deployed or the costs involved but over the gender of the staff assigned. Was this hostile zone suitable for a woman? Would her style of dress and length of hair place her at greater risk than her male colleagues? Was her flak jacket too heavy for her to run out of harm's way? And the unspoken debate about the likelihood of a female media colleague being harassed, sexually assaulted or raped while in a war zone.

The remarkable talent of female war correspondents such as the BBC's Kate Adie, CNN's Christiane Amanpour and Lara Logan of CBS News has moved this debate into the shadows in recent years, but as they and their hundreds of counterparts report daily from the world's trouble spots the issues of women

in harm's way remains a crucial consideration for media bosses and their assignment desks. This point has been driven harshly home with some terrifying examples of our female colleagues being intimidated and assaulted, none more so than the dreadful attack on Lara Logan in Cairo in 2011.

This book is the first that addresses the welfare of our female co-workers through the eyes of the reporters themselves, many of whom offer practical advice on their own survival. It is a powerful story about journalistic passion to tell the story and a searing reminder of the additional dangers that women are prepared to face.

Chris Cramer
Editor at Large, Reuters News
Honorary President, International News Safety Institute

"Man's timid heart is bursting with the things he must not say,
For the Woman that God gave him isn't his to give away;
But when the hunter meets with husbands, each confirms the other's tale –
The female of the species is more deadly than the male."

– Rudyard Kipling, 'The Female of the Species'

foreword

By Lara Logan

I can't feel them anymore. Their hands. The tearing.

It is just the memory.

But that's enough. The memory and everything that comes with it.

I do not really understand how I survived that night in Tahrir Square last February. In my work, the people I have seen overwhelmed by a mob all ended up dead. And it does not take long when you are fighting two hundred to three hundred men in a fury of bloodlust, to realize that your strength is leaving your body and there is truly nothing you can do to stop it.

I remember begging for my life. I remember giving up. I remember fighting back. I remember accepting my death. And I remember clearly, making a decision to go down fighting with my last breath.

I remember everything.

And I now know how easy it is to die. Not in an intellectual way, more of a visceral, carnal understanding that obliterates all light.

I know what fear really is, what it feels like when it seeps into the fibre of your being and like your skin, you can't tear it off or be free of it.

And I know now that I will fight for my life, even when I am certain it is futile and will not change the outcome. I will do that because it will be the last thing I do, that defining moment of my death, that will tell my children everything about who I am and why I left them to travel thousands of miles, to tell the story of a people they may never know or understand.

It's not much of a substitute. Instead of having a mother, they will have the knowledge that their mother never gave up on them.

But in the end, all we have is who we are.

Opposite page: Egyptian protesters run during clashes with men in plain clothes and as soldiers fire into the air in front of the state security headquarters in downtown Cairo March 6, 2011. ©REUTERS/Amr Abdallah Dalsh

But in the end, all we have is who we are... It's the one thing not even three hundred baying men could take from me that night.

It's the one thing not even three hundred baying men could take from me that night.

This book is inspired by what happened to me in that square in Egypt. It is meant to examine what we can do, how we can prepare, what we should know before traveling as journalists into situations that can potentially take our lives, or wound us mortally, or deprive us of our dignity.

It is important that we as women doing dangerous work in hostile places are equipped with knowledge and foresight. Knowing how important it is to stay on your feet in a mob, meant that every time my legs stumbled or gave way or were dragged down, I fought my way back up, saying over and over in my mind, "you have to stay on your feet or you will die". Somehow, somewhere, like a light in the back of your brain, your training and experience kick in, even in the midst of that chaos.

But what cannot be taught or trained, is the knowledge of who you are. That is the light that will guide you to recovery in the dark months or years that follow. That is the light that showed me so clearly how important it was to speak out and not to hide.

I want the world to know that I am not ashamed of what happened to me. I want everyone to know I was not simply attacked – I was sexually assaulted. This was, from the very first moment, about me as a woman. But ultimately, I was just a tool. This was about something bigger than all of us – it was about what we do as journalists. That ancient tactic of terrifying people into submission or silence.

I do not believe it should stop or deter women from doing this kind of work. Or traveling to such places.

There is no real escape from the realities of life, no matter where you are.

But I do feel strongly that a standard was set in my case by a company, my company: CBS News. And that standard is now very clear: you have a duty to stand by your employees, an unconditional, honest, unwavering duty.

We should all be very grateful for that, as the importance cannot be overstated.

Sexual violence – rape – is a unique, humiliating weapon. It is used to great effect against both men and women.

And even though we all know deep down that it could, that it might happen to us, if we didn't believe we could somehow escape then we would not head out the door to do our work in places and circumstances where our lives mean nothing and are so easily erased.

Like that black grime you see between the tiles in a damp, neglected bathroom, an attack like this lives with you. The consequences are not to be underestimated or dismissed.

But it can also be washed away.

And the ideal of freedom that drives us as journalists, the freedom of speech that we embody, is what is really at stake.

– Lara Logan, Chief Foreign Affairs Correspondent, CBS News

Opposite page: CBS Correspondent Lara Logan is pictured in Cairo's Tahrir Square moments before she was assaulted. ©CBS News

contents

Reuters photographer Mariana Bazo stands on a flooded street in the devastated town of La Guaira, Venezuela. © REUTERS

introduction

They are wives and mothers, sisters and daughters, colleagues and friends. They come from more than a dozen countries, work in radio, television, newspapers and online, cross five continents and span generations and religions.

They are many things.

But above all they are journalists.

And women.

Their stories cover war and conflict, disaster and civil unrest, corruption and terror. They include episodes of harrowing assault, awe-inspiring bravery, lucky misses and planned escapes.

Their experiences and voices are their own. In compiling, editing and translating them, we have left the contributions as close to the original articles and interviews as possible, in some case changing just a few words for greater clarity.

For every contributor to this book, there are other women who wanted to take part. Some of them could not because of sickness or injury, the physical and emotional toll of their journalism experiences still lying heavy with them.

There are others who had hoped to but could not because of work or family commitments. And there were still more we should have and could have asked.

Their absence is our loss.

This book has been a labour of love from its inception for all of us and we thank each and every contributor to it.

We know that some of the women found writing these accounts to be a very painful process. And we know that many of our contributors underestimate quite how brave and remarkable are their achievements and those of their colleagues.

We salute them.

Photos (L-R): Jomana Karadsheh and Matthew Chance from CNN are evacuated from the Rixos hotel in Tripoli. © REUTERS/Paul Hackett; A man holds a portrait of Russian journalist Anna Politkovskaya. REUTERS/Alexander Natruskin; and Italian hostage Giuliana Sgrena arrives in Rome after being held hostage in Iraq for more than a month. ©REUTERS/Max Rossi

I am very much the understudy to the brave women in this book. I feel immensely privileged to have worked with these ladies in compiling their stories. Stories that have inspired me and terrified me, made me laugh and, in Lara's case, made me cry.

They strike a chord for many reasons. Not least because I too am a journalist.

I joined the International News Safety Institute a couple of months after visiting Haiti as a producer with a London-based television news crew to cover its devastating earthquake.

It was a country I'd fallen in love with six years earlier as a young female journalist, trying to carve out the career I'd dreamt of for as long as I can remember.

In 2004, it was a dangerous and dark place: a curfew, the nightly reminder of a lawlessness that manifested itself in kidnappings, beheadings and rape. My days were spent reporting on this violent vibrant scene. In the evenings, gunfire provided the exotic chorus as we drank local rum in the hills above the chaotic capital, sharing stories and confidences with the motley crew of foreigners who flock to a country on the edge.

It was an adrenalin-fuelled existence. I was naive and ill-prepared. The gunshot across the bow of the Brazilian UN vehicle I was travelling in through the slums tested my reflexes, but not my resolve. I vowed to return to Haiti to tell the story of its people, but when I did everything had changed.

Camped on the runway of the airport in Port-au-Prince in the aftermath of the earthquake, listening to the planes landing with aid, I remember thinking about the lengths to which news people go to shine a light in dark places, to tell the tales of those whose lives are turned upside down by war, disaster and unrest.

Earlier that day, in the hilltops above Petit Goave, close to the epicentre of the earthquake, I had met a little girl whose eyes seared their way into my soul. She had lost her mother. I thought of my little girl back home and I knew then that this was a job for those

Photos (L-R): Italian journalist Maria Grazia Cutuli in Mogadishu. © REUTERS/ANSA/Cristiano Laruffa; Members of the media at the Rixos hotel in Tripoli. © REUTERS/Paul Hackett; and an Iranian state television journalist looks at a brochure of official hairstyles during a ceremony to mark the national Chastity and Hijab day in Tehran. ©REUTERS/Morteza Nikoubazl

braver than me. That news piece helped earn Channel 4 News a BAFTA nomination. I've never been able to watch it.

As I write this introduction, I realise it's almost exactly a year since the incident that gave rise to this book. On February 11, 2011, the news of the sexual attack on Lara Logan opened a new chapter in the issue of the safety of women journalists.

At the International News Safety Institute, we were inundated with requests for advice and tips for women journalists in dangerous situations.

At the time there was no single point of reference.

As we worked to create one, we realised that there could be no "one size fits all" approach to the debate about the safety of women journalists.

Should women be treated differently from their male colleagues? Some women said yes, others said no. Others said no, then secretly admitted they didn't dare say yes, lest it ruin their chances of being deployed to dangerous places.

Were women at greater risk than their male colleagues solely because of their gender? The answer to this depended greatly on the situation and story.

Some of our contributors detail their daily struggle to work in countries where women are barely accepted in the media. Others tell of situations where they felt safer because they were women. Others pay tribute to the men they worked with who also found their safety at risk.

We know women sometimes do need to take additional measures to protect themselves, but more often than not safety issues don't discriminate on the basis of gender. So we have provided a section at the back of the book, giving general safety tips for all journalists and a shorter female-specific section as well.

INSI is honoured to have the support of many brave men and women journalists in the writing of this book. We are immensely grateful for all of the words of advice, encouragement and inspiration.

We would like to thank UN Women and the Stieg Larsson family for their generous donations, which helped with the publishing of the book.

We know women sometimes do need to take additional measures to protect themselves, but more often than not safety issues don't discriminate on the basis of gender.

Special thanks also go to Thomson Reuters, which supplied many of the photographs that illustrate the articles and supplement those images provided by the women themselves. Colleagues there provided invaluable assistance throughout the compilation, design and the launch of the book, which Thomson Reuters kindly hosted. We are particularly indebted to Mark Thompson, Shannon Ghannam, Sarah Edmonds and Julia Fuller.

Without the unwavering support of Helena Williams this project would not have seen the light of day. My right-hand woman at INSI, Helena's drive, enthusiasm and patience has been remarkable. We've been fortunate to work with Mary Schrider as designer and also benefit from the wit and wisdom of Caroline Neil, who kept us on the straight and narrow with our safety tips. Thanks to the three of you.

Finally, in my limited experience, journalists are only as good as their support teams. To all those friends, loved ones, family members and colleagues who are always there for us when we are coming from, going to, or working in, dangerous places, thank you.

We apologise for the occasional inaccuracy that this book may contain. We ask you to accept any in the spirit in which they were written.

– Hannah Storm, Deputy Director, INSI

Another group of men gathered around us... It was time to leave.

caroline wyatt

The atmosphere was one of celebration as we drove into the northern Afghan town of Kunduz just as it was liberated from the Taliban, on a hot late autumn day in 2001. It must have been just after noon when BBC camerawoman Julie Ritson and I found ourselves filming on the dusty main square, after being taken down to see Taliban prisoners in the foetid main jail; the ones who had so far escaped being shot or beaten.

Both of us wore long scarves to cover our hair, and long-sleeved shirts and trousers, making sure that every inch of flesh was covered. But we were soon surrounded by hundreds of Afghans – and not a single woman among them. Our male colleagues had gone to film elsewhere, and while the crowd seemed friendly, we began to feel uneasy. It was hard for us to move, and we seemed to be the focus of everyone's attention.

Julie continued to film, but the town was becoming tense. There were reports of fighting still going on elsewhere in the town. We tried to find a side road to film our piece to camera, and for a while the attention faded. But then another group of men gathered around us, this time poking and shouting. It was time to leave.

Our young translator Nawzir gently helped clear the way and talk us through the crowd and back to the car. It was only 200 or so metres away, but it felt like a mile. All we could feel was eyes on us everywhere, and just as the skies above were turning deep blue in the dusk, the celebratory atmosphere had also darkened.

We could see old scores being settled around us, as groups of men began confrontations with others. They

An Afghan policeman checks around a guesthouse after it was attacked by suicide bombers in Kunduz. © Reuters/ Wahdat Afghan

Nobody can guarantee your safety in all situations at all times. But using common sense, being prepared, and remaining watchful at all times... can save your life.

didn't want that to be filmed. Definitely time to drive back to the relative safety of our high-walled Afghan house, some 30 miles away.

Just 17 or so, with an ever-ready megawatt smile and rudimentary self-taught English, Nawzir was our lifeline throughout our time with the Northern Alliance. Like most of those in the town of Khodja Bauhouddin, where we had set up our main base, he found it baffling but rather entertaining that two women were there without fathers, brothers or uncles to protect us. "Why are you not married?" he would ask. "Does your father know you are here? And did he and your brothers let you come on your own?"

"Yes," we told him, and explained that at the age of 33 in England, it wasn't so uncommon not to be married – and also quite normal for women to travel without their families, with no stain on our honour.

So in the absence of our own families, Nawzir took it upon himself to take care of us and our honour, though he patiently explained that in the unusual circumstances, those we encountered would simply have to treat us as they would foreign men. We were too inexplicable otherwise.

Nawzir talked us out of many uncomfortable situations in the weeks to come. When a cameraman was killed during a robbery in the house near ours, and we needed to negotiate our way out quickly, Nawzir did the talking. That time, the danger wasn't to do with being female, but foreign and – by local standards – rich.

Yet while being foreign, female journalists in Afghanistan might have been a disadvantage in some ways, it was also an advantage on many occasions. We were welcomed into homes which no foreign male correspondent was allowed into, and we were privileged to hear and film the stories of women of the north in a way none of our male colleagues could.

And perhaps we brought a different perspective to the war: a little less focus on the bombs and bullets, and more on what the end of the Taliban's rule in the north would mean for the families we met, and for their future.

Julie and I had found being female a similar advantage in Chechnya in earlier years, not least because the Chechen families and Russian soldiers we were filming in Grozny saw us as no threat. It was the same in Iraq in 2003, as we drove into the newly liberated

town of Basra in southern Iraq. The main danger from the cheering crowds of Iraqis on that first day was an exuberant festival of bottom-pinching as we got out of our car to film, although there – as in Kabul and elsewhere – our male colleagues were not entirely immune from similar attention.

But in later days, some of that welcome had already turned sour, as expectations of what western troops – and by extension, western camera crews – could do for the people of Basra were not met. Knowing when our welcome had worn out during filming on the streets, or when it was time to lower our profile

For women journalists, it remains vital to think about what you wear and how you come across to people in cultures where women's place in public life is very different...

by going inside or somewhere quieter, was a vital part of our survival skills, along with sound advice from the security adviser who travelled with us.

Likewise, listening to our local translators or producers also proved a lifeline in many situations, when their antennae for when it was time to go or duck into a side-street for a little while were almost always more acute than our own.

Both Julie and I have also been lucky to work for a big news-gathering organisation which takes safety seriously, for its male and female employees alike, particularly in war-zones abroad. Some of that is down to bitter experience. The belief that it will 'never happen to us' as journalists has been proved wrong on too many occasions during the wars of the past decades, and in countries where both foreign and local journalists have become targets in a way they may not have been in earlier years.

The 'hostile environment' safety courses we must do before being sent to a conflict zone, or to cover earthquakes and other natural disasters, include basic first aid training and practical advice on how to handle crowds or riots. Such courses are invaluable, whether you are an experienced old hack who's seen it all

before or new and keen to be deployed abroad. That basic first aid might save a colleague's life, or at least keep them breathing until medical help can be found. And likewise, advice on body language and how to talk your way out of a hostile crowd has proved its worth on countless occasions.

Nobody can guarantee your safety in all situations at all times. But using common sense, being prepared, and remaining watchful at all times – even when engrossed in gathering interviews and pictures on a tight deadline – can save your life.

The basics apply to all journalists working in potentially dangerous places: watching out for your colleagues, and agreeing what time you'll be back at base or at a rendezvous point, making sure you have a Thuraya or satellite phone or mobile with enough battery charged, and taking enough food and water to last if you're out longer than expected, as well as parking the car facing outwards, so that you can drive out straight away if necessary.

For women journalists, it remains vital to think about what you wear and how you come across to people in cultures where women's place in public life is very different, whether that means wearing a headscarf and covering up pretty much from head to toe, or ensuring that male and female members of your team sleep in different rooms.

When working as a freelance or on your own, it's always better to find other journalists to travel with or a trusted translator/driver who knows the place and people – and whose advice you are prepared to listen to, even if it sometimes isn't what you want to hear. No story is worth a life, and knowing when to leave is every bit as important as knowing when to stay to gather the news.

Caroline Wyatt *was appointed BBC Defence Correspondent in October 2007, covering defence for BBC News for TV, radio and BBC Online. Her brief includes wider strategic issues, as well as coverage of the NATO campaign in Afghanistan and the work of British forces elsewhere. She is an occasional presenter for BBC Radio 4's Saturday PM programme, and has presented R4* From Our Own Correspondent, *R4* The World This Weekend *and the World Service radio programmes* Newshour *and* Europe Today.

Did I benefit from being a woman journalist in the civil war in Pattani? … it was easier to talk to local people without them becoming suspicious.

nita roshita

I guess my most exciting and adrenaline-filled experience was when I was in Pattani, Southern Thailand, in May 2007. I was covering stories about the civil war deep in the south of Thailand. Sporadic fighting happened in three provinces: Yala, Narathiwat and Pattani. The Thai army had 30,000 troops all over these provinces, while the number of Muslim insurgents was unknown. It was my first time on the battlefield of civil war.

Did I benefit from being a woman journalist in the civil war in Pattani? I don't think I did much, to be honest – but as a woman, it was easier to talk to local people without them becoming suspicious. When I talked to a Muslim source, I would use my hijab or headscarf to respect their beliefs, and when I talked to a Buddhist source, I didn't use it. Hardliner people are also quite nice and polite when they talk to women – for example, my passport and bag were never checked when I passed through checkpoints, while other male visitors got checked (of course, I only identified myself as a journalist to my sources). I was there for five days – and a few hours after I arrived in Bangkok, my colleague, a male journalist from Time Magazine, and a photographer were bombed in the same location I had been in.

In July 2007 I was in Sidoarjo, East Java, helping a friend cover stories about mud caused by drilling. We were lucky enough to be able to visit the first crater of mud – but it smelt awful and we both didn't use anything to cover our faces or noses. We didn't prepare ourselves, when we should have thought about it in the first place.

Based on my experiences in the field, I just have to make sure that wherever I stay, the sanitation is good. Women need to have a clean toilet and bathroom in the field, especially during menstruation – it's a basic need.

While working at KBR68H, I never felt that I was treated differently from my male colleagues. We have the same

Opposite page: Armed security personnel walk among Thai Buddhist and Muslim passengers on the train they have secured between troubled Yala and Pattani provinces in southern Thailand. © REUTERS/Damir Sagolj

My editor said it would be easier for a woman to get information out of somebody, compared to our male colleagues.

by being sent to talk to Pollycarpus Budihari Priyanto – the pilot who was jailed for the murder of human rights activist Munir Said Thalib. My editor said it would be easier for a woman to get information out of somebody, compared to our male colleagues. But I didn't see this as a negative thing – in fact, I see being able to gather important information easily a benefit to us women.

I did have safety training in March 2008 in Lembang, West Java, by the International News Safety Institute. I was trained in first-aid and how to deal with demonstrations and bomb attacks, but there was no specific training for women journalists' safety.

Here are some tips based on my experiences – they are just small things to prepare and can be used by female or male journalists:

- Make sure you have a trustworthy person with you to help you find the right fixers, sources to talk to and safe places to stay.

- Bring the right kind of equipment to cover stories – in my case, the recording device I chose was very light, and it was not obvious that it was a MiniDisc. Don't bring a normal sized microphone – choose a black clip-on one instead, so you can put it on your

tasks to do and work the same shift patterns, and are treated the same. KBR68H has taken gender issues seriously. There was one time when our news policy was against the anti-pornography law that was upheld in the parliament, and several female journalists and I got threats and verbal abuse from from those who were pro the article, mostly radical Muslims. They said we were not good women since we were against the article that they had called to protect women – yeah right!

But as women, sometimes we got used by our editor to get more information from sources. I was 'used'

backpack or on your shirt. Not many people feel comfortable talking to a microphone, especially in very tense situations.

- This might not be a big thing, but it's very useful to have a black backpack to bring with you wherever you go. You will never know when trouble might happen, and your recorder and all your notes could be destroyed. The black colour is to disguise your clip-on microphone if you are doing undercover stories.

- Always use an earphone to make sure you have recorded all of your interview and the ambiance, as you might not be able to come back to the same place again.

Nita Roshita has worked as a radio journalist in Jakarta, Indonesia, since 2002. She first worked for KBR68H and was transferred to Green Radio 89.2 FM in 2008 – the only radio station in Indonesia that focuses on environmental issues. She was awarded a Southeast Asian Press Alliance (SEAPA) scholarship in 2007, which led her to cover the discrimination of Muslim students in southern Thailand.

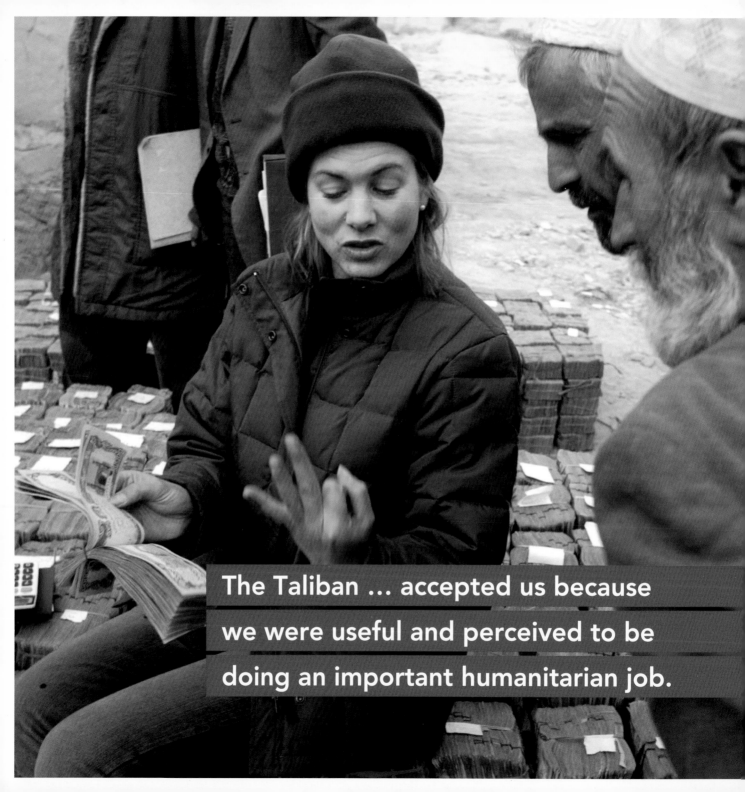

The Taliban ... accepted us because we were useful and perceived to be doing an important humanitarian job.

lucy morgan edwards

I worked in both Afghanistan and Pakistan over a period of six years – from the height of the Taliban period in 2000 to the end of 2005. During that time the security situation revolutionized, for the worse. I worked for aid agencies, and the UN, as an election monitor, a freelance journalist and a political advisor to the EU Ambassador. As such, my work required me to travel independently throughout the country and it was important to understand the factors that affected my security. Aside from the overall security environment, which it is always important to monitor, my personal security could also be affected by the decisions which I made as an individual.

My first job was in Kandahar just over a year before September 11, 2001. This was the height of the Taliban regime and al Qaeda were in the city, though grudgingly accepted by the locals. However disdainful the Taliban might be about foreign aid agencies, they accepted us because we were useful and perceived to be doing an important humanitarian job. At that time the country, after 22 years of war, was also in the grip of a drought which had forced people off their lands and into refugee camps. Our projects, though principally aimed at water supply, targeted the most vulnerable in society (eg widows) and community based projects. They enabled Afghans to have a say in the design of the projects and to select the beneficiaries. This contributed to our security as aid workers. Sadly in the last 10 years the increasing militarization of aid work (ie aid workers living on bases) has meant that aid workers are often no longer perceived by insurgents as impartial but seen as a 'party to the conflict' (ie taking sides). As such, they have become a target.

Opposite page: Lucy Morgan Edwards along with Afghan officials verifies old banknotes that are prepared to be burnt in Kabul December 9, 2002. © REUTERS/Radu Sigheti

In those days before 9/11, for example, we were not allowed to carry armed guards or guns in our UN vehicles. This was considered inducing oneself to being a target. Now, that has all changed. We were also able to travel throughout most of the country by car because this was a period of relative stability.

My security at that stage was also a function of how I dressed and behaved. I tried to fit in with local cultural norms to the extent that I dressed in long cloaks if going out on the streets and wore the headscarf. We were not allowed to walk alone and if I made the short trip between the house I lived in and our office (1 block), I had to be accompanied by a male staff member. This was more for cultural reasons than security. Kandahar has always been a conservative area so this was not just because it was under Taliban rule. At this stage our only communication with the outside world (apart from the BBC World Service on my shortwave radio) was by handheld walkie-talkie or by Codan radio to Islamabad. This meant that all communication was essentially public and it was easy for one's whereabouts to be tracked. There were no mobile phones and only one landline at the 'Gen'ral Post office'.

When I returned to work in Afghanistan during the war I worked as an election monitor and freelance journalist. As I made more friends, so it became easier to travel around. I would cadge lifts or go by taxi or mini bus. At this stage the only email (unless you were with a big press agency with a sat phone which at that stage looked like a laptop) you had to cross town by taxi or with your hired driver to the InterContinental hotel which had an internet café. I learnt a lot from other journalists, but most left for Iraq in late 2002. I

feelings about what was going on. They were national figures but within the year that I met them two of the brothers had been assassinated. I think I was given better access because, as a woman, I was not deemed a threat and my interest in them was a reason I was made welcome. Though my proximity to them possibly contributed to my safety in the East of the country, I still travelled independently into the tribal areas, Nuristan, and back and forth over the Torkham border crossing into Pakistan with no problems.

stayed in houses with other foreigners but also stayed with Afghan families, in particular, the family I wrote about in my book, *The Afghan Solution: The inside story of Abdul Haq, the CIA and how western hubris lost Afghanistan.* This enabled me to gain a very different perspective of the conflict and to learn their

Lucy Morgan Edwards *is a former Political Advisor to the EU Ambassador in Kabul with responsibility for civil military affairs, narcotics and security sector reform. During her seven years in the region she worked for the UN in Kandahar at the height of the Taliban regime, was an election monitor and a correspondent for the* Economist *and* Daily Telegraph, *and the initial researcher for the International Crisis Group on Transitional Justice Issues.*

She is author of The Afghan Solution: The Inside Story of Abdul Haq, the CIA and How Western Hubris Lost Afghanistan. *She has presented papers of Afghanistan at Chatham House, the Royal Society of Asia Affairs and the Frontline Club in London.*

THE RIGHT TO WRITE?

In this business we are unarmed… so the only weapon we have is a pen.

duruthu edirimuni chandrasekera

I used to be a banker, but that became claustrophobic. My intention was to do something important – I wanted to make my mark. One of the reasons I wanted to go into journalism is because we are perceived as a tough breed, especially women financial journalists, because finance is largely supposed to be a male thing.

Sri Lanka is developing, and I deal with reporting on the emerging market and economy. Many listed companies in Sri Lanka don't want to have negative stuff written about them because it will affect their share price, but my job is to find out the dirt, and to get it published.

Being a financial journalist is a risky business. It's taken a long time to build up trust and reputation, and it was more difficult because I am a woman. You have to deal with businessmen and tycoons, and you handle very valuable corporate information.

In this business we are unarmed and we don't have any particular safety training, so the only weapon we have is a pen. Businessmen do have some respect for us, but it's like a double-edged sword.

I've been threatened by those I've written about. And on one occasion, when I tried to stand up to persistent abuse and threats against my life and livelihood, my husband and colleagues suggested I shouldn't react, that I shouldn't cross swords with those in power and that I was being threatened because I was a female journalist.

The challenge of being a female financial journalist is enormous. As journalists, women can't go to some areas that male colleagues can, because they say it is unsafe for women.

Opposite page: A woman takes part in a vigil for missing journalist Prageeth Eknaligoda in Colombo © REUTERS/Andrew Caballero-Reynolds

There is also a lot of prejudice when it comes to female journalists. People think we can charm men to get our stories, and men, especially business tycoons, can be very suave. They say things like, "Why don't you come to lunch? Why don't you come to dinner? Why don't you come for cocktails?' – and they think we'll fall for it, and so be under obligation, as a lot of journalists still are.

In Sri Lanka, many people think that if you go for drinks with somebody you can't write anything negative against them. They think that we will only write positive stuff after cocktails and food. A lot more can be done to change the culture of our profession: in training, etc. At my desk, we are told not to accept gifts and things like that, which is a step in the right direction.

I am very serious about my job – journalism is about telling the truth to people. If I write the truth, at times it's perceived as negative journalism. Many newspapers have been refused advertising by corporates and individuals because of so-called negative things written about them, so there is pressure.

The best advice I can give to any woman journalist is to not be intimidated, don't do any favours for anyone, and to know who you are as a person.

As a female journalist, you have to be aware that this job means you have to make sacrifices. Thankfully my husband is very supportive and proud of what I do, whereas my parents were very unsupportive at the start, thinking it's not a proper job.

I feel that women journalists shouldn't be treated any differently to men – it's important that they are treated exactly the same. The best advice I can give to any woman journalist is to not be intimidated, don't do any favours for anyone, and to know who you are as a person. You have to write what is, and let people have their own opinions about it.

–Interviewed by Helena Williams

Duruthu Edirimuni Chandrasekera *has been a journalist for 9 years. She is a financial journalist for the* Business Times, *the financial and business arm of the* Sunday Times, *in Sri Lanka. As an investigative business journalist, she often reports on white-collar crime, as well as loopholes in the legal system. By doing so she helps negate white-collar crime, thereby boosting corporate governance in the business sector.*

Like our male colleagues, our main concerns are staying alive and keeping our limbs and brains intact.

tina susman

The first question my rescuers asked after they pulled me from the room where I'd been held captive in Somalia was: "Did they rape you?" They seemed surprised when I said no. The assumption was that any woman held hostage for three weeks must have been sexually assaulted.

People still assume I was raped, but they won't ask in such a direct fashion. Instead, they say (usually in hushed tones): "Were you mistreated?" or "Did they abuse you?" Still, the meaning is clear, and the questions and the way they are posed underscore a couple of things: the rather morbid fascination people have with the idea of a tough female journalist falling victim to sexual assault on assignment; and the aversion to saying "rape," as if it were shameful or something to be kept secret. Like my rescuers, they seem surprised – and I suspect many don't believe me – when I tell them that I was not raped. They seem even more surprised to hear that rape was the least of my worries during my kidnapping, just as it has never figured prominently on the list of concerns I've had in the countless countries, wars, and disasters I've covered since. I worried – and worry – about my plane or helicopter being shot down; being trampled in a stampede;

being hit by a stray bullet; getting kidnapped again; or stepping on a landmine. I even worry about a giant insect crawling into my sleeping bag.

Perhaps because rape is not a job-specific threat like bombs and missiles (and giant bugs), it doesn't occupy my mind on assignment the way those other threats do. Based on conversations with other female journalists, I don't think I'm unusual. Like our male colleagues, our main concerns are staying alive and keeping our limbs and brains intact.

But as long as most assigning editors are male, rape will always be one of their big worries. Terry Anderson, a former AP colleague who was held hostage in Beirut for 7 years, told me this when we met some years ago. He said it was a male editor's greatest fear: that a woman work-

Opposite page: Somali children dispersed by UN Pakistani peacekeepers in front of Mogadishu airport. © REUTERS/Corinne Dufka

Safety isn't contained in a medical kit or a flak jacket...It involves a lot of common sense and...things that more journalists need to be equipped with before they're sent on assignment.

ing for him could be sexually assaulted. That's a problem, because as long as there are editors viewing their female correspondents as potential rape victims, it's bound to affect staffing decisions.

What irks me about the discussion of sexual assaults of female journalists is the double-standard that often emerges in the conversation – mainly from non-journalists, but sometimes from journalists themselves. When my (many) male colleagues have been killed or injured on assignment, I've rarely heard anyone say of men: "They're too macho and always run toward the action, so maybe we shouldn't send guys into war zones." Yet when a female is sexually assaulted, the questions immediately arise as to why a woman was there in the first

place, and whether it is wise to have a woman reporting from a dangerous place.

Rather than questioning the wisdom of sending women into potentially perilous duty or worrying for their safety, editors and news organizations should focus on preparing women (and men) for the threat of sexual violence and helping them avoid it. One of my favorite tools to travel with when I was based in sub-Saharan Africa, for example, was a doorstop which I'd shove under my hotel room door when I was in the room. It emitted an unbelievably loud shriek if anyone tried to open the door. I still consider it one of the best rape-prevention tools ever, in part because nobody could use it against me (unlike a taser gun or pepper-spray, for instance). I

ters, and less like an independent Western woman for whom they would have less regard.

I wish some of my editors could have passed on some of these tips. They didn't, so I figured things out on my own. It shouldn't be that way. Safety isn't contained in a medical kit or a flak jacket, which most news outlets happily hand out. It involves a lot of common sense and sometimes something as simple as a door stop – things that more journalists need to be equipped with before they're sent on assignment.

also learned to adjust my back story to fit the circumstances. If I had to pretend to be married with children to be safe, I invented a husband and kids' names. If I had to pretend to be a devout Christian, a Republican, a Democrat, or Swiss, I did it. As far as my kidnappers knew, I was married with three children – something that made me appear more like their own mothers and sis-

Tina Susman *was the* Los Angeles Times *bureau chief in Baghdad from 2007 until 2009, when she returned to New York to be a national correspondent. Prior to joining the* Times *she worked for the Associated Press and Newsday. She spent 11 years in sub-Saharan Africa, during which she covered the fall of the apartheid in South Africa, the Rwandan genocide, the Somali famine and war, and conflicts in Liberia, Sudan, Sierra Leone, Nigeria and Angola, among others. After returning to New York in 2001 to be a Newsday national writer, she continued to do overseas work amidst national reporting, including Pakistan after 9/11, Darfur, the London metro bombings, the tsunami, Haiti, and the Athens Olympics. She also covered the Michael Jackson trial – not foreign, but otherworldly. Since returning to the U.S. in 2009 she has focused on national news with occasional overseas forays, including to Haiti to cover the 2010 earthquake.*

Giving up my job was but a small sacrifice if it meant Egyptians would be free…

shahira amin

I have never thought of myself as a "female journalist". I think of myself as a journalist full-stop.

Being a woman has not stopped me from covering the Sharm el Sheikh bomb attacks in 2005 or the 2008-2009 Israeli assault on Gaza. My bosses would have certainly preferred to send one of the channel's male reporters to cover such gruesome tragedies. But none were available and so they – reluctantly and apologetically – assigned me the tasks instead.

I of course jumped at the chance: my adventurous spirit and my journalistic sense have always driven me to 'go the extra mile' for a worthy story. And that is perhaps why I have found myself on several occasions in perilous situations . There were times when I did wish I were home lying on my living room sofa watching TV in airconditioned comfort. But such thoughts were merely quick flashes that were almost instantly wiped away by the excitement of an exhilirating experience.

Like the time I was aboard a helicopter in the middle of the night in stormy weather in southern Thailand trying to escape Islamist rebels who had threatened to bomb our hotel resort because we were in the company of the enemy (in this case, the much detested Buddhist government). Or the night I slept on a hard bench braving freezing temperatures in a makeshift army tent to witness the historic solar eclipse the following day on the Matruh-Libyan border. I can now look back and smile when I think about my 'daring' experiences, but at the time, I wasn't so sure they would leave me totally unscathed.

I now truly believe in the saying : what doesn't kill you makes you stronger. My experiences have indeed toughened me and I am not one to be easily intimidated.... Not even by Mubarak's brutal security forces nor by the ruthless ousted regime itself.

Opposite page: A woman walks past a mural depicting a woman with an eye patch near Tahrir Square in Cairo. © REUTERS/Amr Abdallah Dalsh

A boy prays in Tahrir Square. © REUTERS/Amr Abdallah Dalsh

And that perhaps explains why I was able to quit my job in protest at Egyptian state television's coverage of the mass uprisings last year. Many other equally indignant journalists stopped short of publicly rebelling because they had feared a backlash from the Mubarak regime. Others could not walk out because they wanted to hang on to their jobs at any cost. Neither a backlash nor the need to earn a livelihood the only way I know how, prevented me from what many have since described as a 'courageous whistleblowing act' – one that significantly contributed to the downfall of the regime.

To be honest, it had been a spur of the moment decision. I had not carefully thought it out or planned it. All that went through my head at the time was the fact that history was in the making in my own backyard and my hands were tied. I was not able to take a camera crew to Tahrir to tell the world what was happening just a few

meters away from the state television building where I worked. To add insult to injury, I was being asked to give viewers a distorted picture of what was happening. The directives issued by the Ministry of Interior and handed to us in the form of press releases clearly described the pro-democracy activists in Tahrir Square as "foreign agents "and "traitors". I had been to Tahrir and had seen for myself that this was a popular all-inclusive movement. These protesters were demanding "freedom, justice and an end to corruption." I had yet to meet one Egyptian who did not agree with those very legitimate demands.

The breakpoint for me was watching on television the men on horseback and on camels storm into the square to attack the activists. This was like a scene from medieval times. It was no secret that state television had always been and continues to be the mouthpiece of the government...how could I continue to speak on behalf of a regime that resorts to such measures to silence voices of dissent? That was the one thought that went through my head as I walked into Tahrir on the morning of the 3rd of February 2011 (the day after the camel attack)and stayed there until the day Mubarak was forced out.

I have no regrets. Giving up my job was but a small sacrifice if it meant Egyptians would be free and would be able to live in dignity. Others, much younger than me had sacrificed their lives for the same cause.

I am now working as a journalist on a freelance basis contributing to various foreign networks and media organisations . I feel freer and happier than I have ever felt before – without the stifling restrictions and heavy censorship I had faced during my 22 years as a senior anchor/correspondent working for state-run Nile TV.

And just as I did back then, I continue to challenge those in authority. At the end of May, I broke the story on the virginity checks carried out by the military on 17 female protesters who had been arrested on the 9th of March – almost one month after the end of the mass uprisings. I had interviewed a researcher for Amnesty International who told me that the human rights violations were worse today than they were under Mubarak. I decided to take the accusations to the Supreme Council of the Armed Forces (SCAF) and give them a chance to respond. The senior general I met who spoke to me on condition of anonymity admitted for the first time that the tests had been conducted in "self defence".

"We decided to carry out the virginity checks to prevent these girls from accusing us of sexually assaulting them afterwards. We had to prove they weren't virgins anyway," he explained.

Next morning, when my story was posted online, all hell broke loose. There were numerous tweets and several websites that alleged I had been summoned for questioning by the military prosecutor. I was never summoned nor interrogated. The allegations were meant to discredit or intimidate me. They did neither. I did however spend several sleepless nights wondering if security agents or Egypt's notorious dawn visitors, would come and break into the house in the early hours.

It was worth it however to hear the military rulers promise activists from Human Rights Watch that they would never again resort to such violations. This, after immense pressure was piled from rights activists inside and outside the country after the story was published.

Being a woman has never stopped me from doing what I considered was the right thing to do...tell the truth and cover the story impartially and objectively no matter what. Mubarak's security men once threatened that "I would disappear from the face of the earth next time I challenged the authorities". The blatant threat had come in response to my coverage of the 2006 massacre by riot police of Sudanese refugees who had staged a sit-in in a public square in Cairo.

I admit I was psychologically traumatised for months afterwards but even then, I refused to be intimidated. It is our duty as journalists – female or male – to tell the public the truth . What difference does it make who tells the story as long as it is told?

Shahira Amin *is an award-winning freelance Egyptian journalist. She worked as Deputy Head of Egypt's state-run Nile TV and was the channel's Senior Anchor/Correspondent, but quit in the early days of the mass uprising that forced out Hosni Mubarak in protest at state tv coverage of the events in Tahrir.*

Shahira now writes for Index on Censorship and CNN.com and produces feature stories for CNN's Inside Africa.She has received recognition from UNICEF for her efforts to improve the status of women and children in her country (2009). She is also winner of the Homes of the Year award 2011 for her ardent defence of human rights and the American University in Cairo's Catalyst for Change Award 2011 for standing up for journalistic ethics.

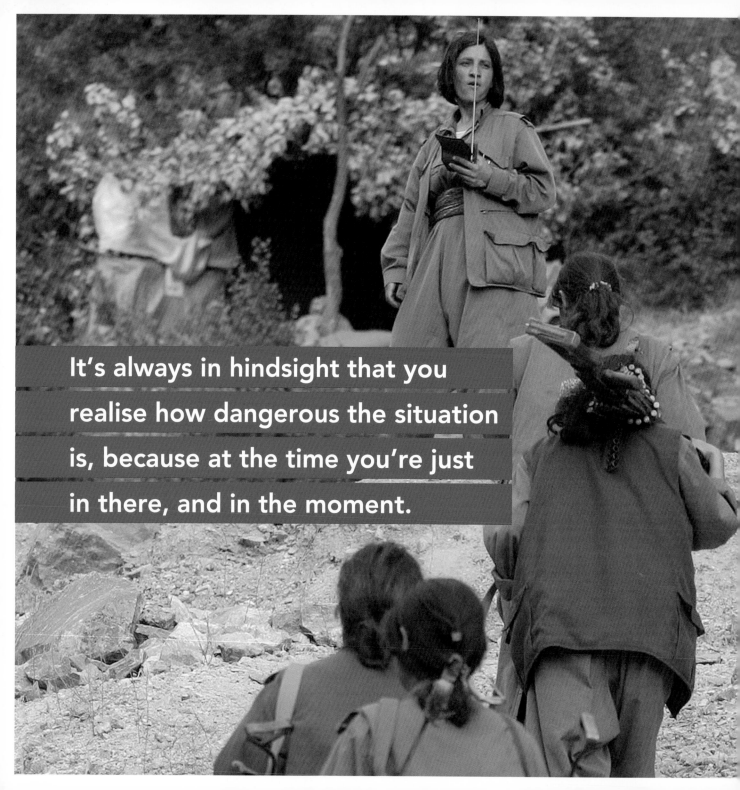

It's always in hindsight that you realise how dangerous the situation is, because at the time you're just in there, and in the moment.

bay fang

It's always in hindsight that you realise how dangerous the situation is, because at the time, you're just in there and in the moment. There are a few different dangerous situations I've been in, for a few different reasons – and not necessarily related to being a woman.

There were a couple times in Northern Iraq when I was with the Kurdish Peshmerga, who were working with the US Special Forces to push back the Iraqi military. We were a handful of journalists and we weren't embedded – we just travelled around with a driver and a translator. We would rush in and drive in to the front lines and just crouch in these foxholes, and try to cover the fighting.

That was the most dangerous place to be. We'd often find ourselves in the crossfire, and there was one journalist who was actually killed because he stepped on a landmine. We went there because we thought that was where the story was.

Whenever I reported in Afghanistan, especially in very rural areas, I would go out with a headscarf out of respect for their cultural norms. I wouldn't wear a burka because it would impinge on me being able to work freely. For the most part, we were seen as a third gender: we weren't held to the same standards as Afghan women, and we weren't seen as western men either. We were just this curiosity. And in a way, because we were seen as a third gender, I felt more protected. I felt people didn't see women as as much of a threat as they did a colleague of mine, who might be an obviously western male. We also had access to local women, while our male colleagues didn't, for the most part – and the local men wanted to talk to us too, because they didn't normally get a chance to talk to women.

But at the same time, there were some really difficult situations. Any time I went out in these rural areas I would be instantly surrounded. If I was walking in a market place, my driver or translator would usually

come with me and act as a bodyguard, because if we stopped and started talking to anyone we would get crowds of hundreds of people surrounding us. Other than my driver or translator, there would usually be some town elder who would appoint themselves as my protector.

I never really felt scared during these scenarios, but I could definitely see how they might turn ugly – especially if you're in an area where there might be a little more anti-American, anti-western feeling. Someone could have easily instigated something that could have caused a mob scene, with me in the middle of it. But it was more harassment, rather than real security issues, that I found bothered me. I've never had a situation where I've felt seriously violated, but I think I was lucky.

Male or a female, you have to use your own judgement as to whether it is more beneficial to be low profile, or to have additional security which might make you stand out. Being a woman, especially in places like Iraq and Afghanistan, makes it easier to be low profile. I'm Chinese American, and look Asian, so if I put on an abaya – especially in the Shi'a areas of Iraq – I would

be able to go out in the middle of the street and people wouldn't look twice at me. Obviously, if the locals were really watching they would know by the way you carried yourself that you weren't local –but still, it was much easier to be under the radar.

After coming back from Afghanistan and Iraq I decided to start doing kung fu and martial arts just so I could easily defend myself. I decided to do that because there was one scenario, which my colleagues still bring up, when we were covering the first day of school in Kabul. It was in 2002, and President Karzai was giving a speech. There was a huge crowd of supporters in the street: it was supposed to be this rewarding experience of seeing these little girls going to school for the first time, and there was a guy behind me who just would not stop grabbing my butt. I tried pushing him off, and finally, I just grabbed his shoulder and knee him in the groin. He looked completely appalled – and immediately stopped!

I've also been on a couple different hostile environment training courses, and I found them useful for certain scenarios that I hope would never happen to me. There was a lot of kidnap training, and defensive

tips

- Don't draw attention to your femininity, especially if you are covering the Muslim world. For your own personal safety, don't wear tight clothing, or perfume.

- Bring an abaya to let you blend in more easily with the local population – even if you don't end up using it, it's nice to know that it might be easier to blend in.

- Use good judgement when you're going to a scene where you might be surrounded by a lot of people. Even if it seems completely benign, it can change very quickly.

- And don't be afraid to raise these issues with your editor.

By all means, editors should send women as much as they send men out to these places – but I do think that women might take it upon themselves to increase their own security measures, and editors should definitely be understanding of this. Even if it's just hiring someone local to go around with the journalist and act as a bodyguard, in addition to having a driver and translator (that's the bare minimum). Having someone smart, who knows the local situation, is really the biggest defence.

I would hope that having a little more expenditure, for the sake of providing additional security, wouldn't deter an editor from sending out a female journalist. A lot of people have been talking about this this year, because of what happened to Lara Logan in Egypt, and I think a lot of female journalists would choose not to raise these issues because of the fear that they might not get sent out. Do not be afraid to raise these issues with your editor.

–Interviewed by Helena Williams

Bay Fang is the incoming Deputy Assistant Secretary of State for Press and Public Diplomacy for Europe in the US State Department. From 2006-2008 she was the diplomatic correspondent for the Chicago Tribune, covering foreign affairs and travelling with the Secretary of State. She was also an adjunct professor of journalism at Georgetown University during this time.

From 2002-2006 she was a correspondent-at-large for US News and World Report magazine, serving as the magazine's chief correspondent in Iraq in 2003-2004, and was Beijing bureau chief for the magazine from 1998-2002. She won the Robert F. Kennedy award in 1999 for her story "China's Stolen Wives," about women who are kidnapped and sold as wives in the Chinese countryside.

driving, and what to do in a mob situation, and how to talk people down - which means calm them down – but it wasn't female specific. I think an explicit mention that there could be some situations in which women are more vulnerable would raise awareness, because I do think that male colleagues might not realise how vulnerable women are in some situations.

Foreign female journalists have an advantage in countries where local women are subject to certain cultural restrictions.

anonymous

I have worked in many different areas of conflict, including Afghanistan, Iraq, Lebanon and Libya, but I do not consider the fundamental dangers in these areas to be any different for a female or a male journalist. On the front line, for example, a woman is just as likely to be shot or hit by indiscriminate shelling as a man. She can just as easily be the victim of a bombing or an IED [Improvised Explosive Device] strike. Weapons do not discriminate between the sexes.

The risks of kidnap are the same for both men and women, as are health risks and the dangers of accident or injury. I am frustrated by the frequent assumption that women are more vulnerable than men in 'dangerous' places, because in my experience I do not believe this to be the case. Yes, working as a journalist can be risky, and these hazards are everywhere – not just in areas of conflict. Anyone can be unlucky – male or female. True, women need to be more alert in certain scenarios, but most safety decisions for women, as for men, are simply based on common sense. That, of course, does not guarantee that nothing will go wrong, but it helps.

If anything, foreign female journalists have an advantage in countries where local women are subject to certain cultural restrictions. It is rare for a foreign woman to be subjected to the same set of rules, as she is usually considered to be different to local women, almost as if she is an 'honorary male'. She is therefore usually excused from any cultural restraints. This gives female reporters the best of both worlds, because not only are we free to do our work, but we are not subject to the restrictions which male reporters face while speaking to women. Of course, sensitivities still apply, and not every woman wishes to be filmed or interviewed regardless of the gender of the reporter – but a foreign female journalist automatically has much better access to local women and their stories than a man. In many countries, a male reporter cannot always approach a local woman to speak to her, film or photograph her. But as a foreign woman I have always found it much easier to talk freely to both men and women.

Libyan women march in support of the women who were raped during the recent war. © REUTERS/Mohammed Salem

A woman takes pictures from behind a barrier separating women from men at Taghyeer (Change) Square in Yemen. © REUTERS/Khaled Abdullah

I am often asked how hard it must be to work in these conservative countries as a woman – a question which always irritates me because of its prejudice and pre-conceived ideas. Rather than experiencing difficulties, I find that as a foreign woman, I am treated with great respect in these places. In most Arab and many Asian counties, hospitality is a key part of the culture – which means that international guests are usually treated with courtesy, but as a woman I have usually been shown even greater kindness. People want to go the extra mile to help solve a problem, are eager to assist carrying heavy equipment and very often invite me to family homes for a meal. Women are generally treated with less suspicion and trusted more easily than men, which can be a great advantage when working on a

story and trying to understand more about the country you are working in.

Obviously cultural common sense and basic respect is essential to good relations, despite the immunity a foreign female may have from local customs or restrictions. These all depend on the country, region, religion or even the family or individual person concerned. There are no hard and fast rules, but obviously a woman should pay attention to clothing in conservative cultures: avoiding bare flesh by wearing long sleeves, loose trousers and headscarf where appropriate. I am amazed how many female western reporters I see wearing short-sleeved T-shirts, or tight jeans, in a religiously conservative environment. It is not advisa-

Common sense also applies to behavior – I would check first before going somewhere where I see no other women.

ble. Look around you and see what other women wear. Showing any area of your body which local women do not show themselves will attract attention. If you do not wish men to stare more than they already do – because they will if you are a foreign, female and waving a camera around – then cover it up. If men have never seen something before other than in a bootleg DVD or a magazine, they give a long hard look.

Bear in mind that you will always be a foreigner and a bit 'different' to local women, so no matter what you wear you will probably attract some attention in public, particularly if you are interviewing or filming. But in my opinion, trying to blend in by going for the all-out 'burka look' does not help either. Local people know you are foreign and there is no hiding that – and you do actually want to ensure you are perceived as a foreigner and not as a local, otherwise you will miss out on the exemption you need from any cultural restrictions.

Common sense also applies to behavior – I would check first before going somewhere where I see no other women. For example, in certain cultures, I would never walk into a room full of local men uninvited, or without assessing how appropriate it would be first. Some restaurants in very conservative countries are 'men only', or may have a family table tucked away at the back. There is no point in trying to defy that system as it will only attract unwanted attention. I would also urge caution when mixing with male-dom-

inated crowds at rallies or demonstrations. In some Islamic countries, public gatherings have a women's section, which may be a more comfortable area to work in. Under no circumstances would I want to be in a situation where I would be physically enclosed by a crowd of men who are not used to close contact with unknown, especially foreign, women. In the western world, it is normal for men and women to be squeezed shoulder to shoulder on a train, or at a concert or a party. In a more conservative country, this public proximity is unheard of and men could see the presence of a foreign woman in the crowd as a moment of opportunity to 'break the rules' and believe there is a chance to get away with something in the confusion of the masses.

Likewise, when getting into a crowded car or taxi, I would never squeeze on to the back seat full of local men, brushing elbows and thighs. If you are a woman, sit in the back alone and let the men stay in the front, or sit in the front passenger seat if there are men in the back. It is a simple thing to do which saves a lot of trouble. It also shows you understand and respect local culture. If you are paying for the car or taxi, make sure you remain in control. Do not allow the driver to give a lift to 'brothers' or 'uncles' therefore outnumbering you with strange men in the vehicle, and be firm on driving the route you want to go. Many kidnappings happen when a driver is paid off to take a certain road which leads to a trap. If the driver does not

The biggest warning would be regarding western expat men in countries which have religiously conservative cultures. These men are a hidden, unexpected hazard to an unsuspecting foreign female.

do as you ask, or if you are not comfortable, then get out of the taxi where it is safe to do so and walk away. Cars are precious commodities and the driver will not abandon his vehicle in the middle of the street just to chase after a few dollars fare.

While most men in conservative countries are kind and respectful, I am always aware that a foreign woman has a certain sexual mystique. However decent a young local man might appear to be, you should be aware that most youth everywhere have access to the internet, and the stricter the country in religious terms, the more likely you are to find young men surfing porn sites at the back of an internet café – it is naïve to think they do not do so. And you may find those with a more simple attitude to life may view a foreign woman in the same light as a porn star, wrongly believing that all western women must be this way, as they have seen them having rampant sex in a movie.

I find it important, when hiring local male colleagues as translators or fixers, to be clear and firm from the very start that this is a working relationship. While it is normal in these cultures to talk about family, be careful – do not accept any questions about boyfriends, lovers or partners which are actually designed to probe about your sex life or potential for promiscuity. I always make it clear that I am offended if a male translator or driver asks me about such personal mat-

ters. Remember, they cannot behave that way with their own women. Invent a partner if you have to. If you admit to being single when you are slightly older, then there will instantly be a thousand questions, as this is unthinkable in most Islamic cultures. I am usually open about not having a husband as lying becomes complicated in the long run, but I do not tolerate any kind of questioning on the subject. Be very careful here – young local men can often start building ideas in their heads that because you do not have a husband, you must either be promiscuous or desperately in need of a man.

Watch out too for the false love, the marriage proposals from men desperate to live in a western country. I have had more earnest proposals from strangers than I can count – not one of them do I imagine to be genuine. Particularly in war-torn countries, men are anxious to get out and start a new life in Europe or the U.S. A marriage certificate is the easiest way of doing this. The safest way to deal with the situation is not to get involved at any level in the first place.

But for me, the biggest warning would be regarding western expat men in countries which have religiously conservative cultures. These men are a hidden, unexpected hazard to an unsuspecting foreign female. Men working away from home in hazardous areas usually do not have their families with them and believe they can live by a different set of rules. Wedding rings slip off, partners are far away and all but forgotten. These western men think that whatever they do in a foreign country will never be noticed at home, so anything goes: 'what happens on the road, stays on the road'. They are adrenaline-fueled, excited and tense from being in a dangerous conflict zone. They want to let off steam. Many actively seek sex to do so. The problem is, that in countries such as Afghanistan or Iraq, they cannot get anywhere near a local woman. They may never even see, or speak to one, let alone approach her for sex. Prostitution is also less accessible. That leaves us western females as the only easy targets. And there are always far fewer foreign women in conflict zones than men. Those few women are under serious pressure. True, some of these women may also be seeking sex, or to let off steam, but those of us who do not wish to do so can be at risk. Many of these expat men are tough, ex-military types who do not take no for an answer. They may try to charm a woman at first, but take other measures when that does not work. They come from a western culture, and unlike the local men, they are used to getting sex on tap mostly when they want it. Be very, very careful. I would keep a distance at all times, lock hotel rooms and doors and be wary of who you are alone with. Those who you think you are safe with are the ones to watch.

And should anything go wrong – be aware of this. There is probably absolutely nothing you can do about it. Local police and authorities are unlikely to help, as local men who commit sexual offences in these cul-tures usually get away with it, and the woman is instead blamed or punished. People in your home country can not act on a sexual offence which happened on foreign soil. There are no rules for these expat men to play by. Not all will take advantage of this – but there are some who do. Be very careful around them.

a note on body armour

Body armour is usually designed to fit men rather women. I have often been issued with the incorrect size by an employer and more or less told I would have to put up with it as that is all they have available. However, ill-fitting body armour can leave key areas of the body vulnerable – in one case it was so big on me, it exposed the area of my chest and heart, which seemed rather pointless. Oversized body armour also restricts movement, which is a haz-ard if you need to run, duck or jump in and out of vehicles in a hurry. It is possible to get body armour tailor made for women, but it is expen-sive and you are unlikely to be issued this as standard by your employer. For some strange reason you are supposed to suddenly adopt the size and shape of a man.

Being a woman journalist in Pakistan is in itself a great achievement.

shumaila jaffery

During the coverage of the earthquake in 2005, I worked in all the quake hit districts of Kashmir and Khyber Pakhtunkhawa. I still remember in one of the areas, a local mosque's Imam issued a fatwa that a man of faith should not marry women who had been working in quake-hit areas.

Being a woman journalist in Pakistan is in itself a great achievement. Over the years we have seen a greater interest in females in the media industry and for sure their number has been increased, but still the industry is male dominant.

We have seventy plus television channels, but the number of women at top management level is almost zero, at middle management there are a very few, and the majority of them are working in junior positions.

The same is the case with print media, and though there have been and still are women in editors and managers roles, their number is very limited.

Particularly in the TV media, women are preferred as sex symbols to add glamour on the screen.

Although all media organizations claim that they are equal opportunity employers, in reality there's still a long way to go to achieve the goal of equal opportunities for women journalists in Pakistan.

Women face bias at all stages in the day-to-day professional routine. As beat reporters, they are considered good for covering "softer stories", and mostly don't get the opportunity to cover hard-core issues.

Most of the media organizations do not have gender policies; a few bigger news organisations claim that

Opposite: A Pakistani refugee in Bangkok. ©REUTERS/Damir Sagolj

comments, they are asked to give "favours" to bosses and colleagues to get a promotion or any other professional benefit which is their right, and at times they are even sexually assaulted.

The majority of such cases are never reported and those that were, then the women had to go through so much pain that they thought it better to remain quiet.

Recently one of my best friends working in a state-owned channel was sexually harassed by her colleague, she talked to general manager at her TV station, but no action was taken against the culprit.

Most of the media organizations do not have rules for maternity leave, many women journalist are forced to quit their careers after getting married or after getting pregnant.

In Pakistan, the worst harassment against women occurs on public transport. So for female reporters, transportation is another challenge. The majority of media organisations do not provide transport to their female staffers, and very few can afford to have their own cars, so most of the time they are at the mercy of public transport, or forced to ride on a bike with their photographers.

they have gender policies, but even that doesn't help much to provide a conducive environment for female journalists because people working in these organisations are hardly even aware of them.

I am lucky that I have not faced any sexual harassment issue, but many of my colleagues have been going through all this. They are subjected to unwelcoming

Working in the field is also very difficult; women journalists have to face nasty comments, looks and attitudes.

If you are working in an urban area with comparatively educated community you are better, but if you are working in Khyber Pakthunkhawa, Balochistan, Interior Sindh, South Punjab or rural Punjab, the environment would be completely different.

And in war zones, or tribal areas women journalists are strongly advised or forced not to work. Access for male reporters is even restricted, but for women journalists they are no-go areas. Although it is primarily for their security, women in Pakistan are deprived of covering big, hard-core international stories solely because of their gender.

Shumaila Jaffery *started her journalism career as a freelance writer. She joined the state-owned Pakistan Television as a reporter and news producer in 2000, and worked there for seven years until she resigned 2007 after becoming frustrated with the channel's editorial restrictions. She joined News Channel Dunya TV the same year, and is currently working there as a senior correspondent and assignment editor. She has covered a broad range of stories, from natural disasters to terrorism.*

I learned very quickly when I moved to India two years ago that crowds in South Asia are a hostile place for women.

anonymous

I learned very quickly when I moved to India two years ago that crowds in South Asia are hostile places for women. I was covering a political rally in Haryana, a state that is sadly notorious for gender-related violence, just a couple of hours from the capital New Delhi. There were three of us – two women and a male photographer – and we decided to leave the rally early as it was tedious and we wanted to beat the traffic.

As we waited on a dusty road for our driver, we were suddenly surrounded for no reason by a group of 50 to 60 men, all staring wildly, and edging closer, to the point where some were just inches away. One threw a stone, and the situation looked unpredictable.

After a few tense moments we finally managed to locate the driver, but to this day I'm convinced that the story would have been uglier if we hadn't had a male colleague with us.

In India or Pakistan, a mob situation is often only minutes away. On another occasion, I went with a female colleague to a crowded market street in Mumbai. A bomb had gone off two days before and we wanted to interview witnesses. Again, we were instantly sur-rounded and, after one bum grab too many, decided we had enough quotes and left.

In South Asia it's often hard to report on the streets without drawing a crowd, and until Lara Logan was attacked in Cairo, I used to dismiss the unabashed staring and constant brushing against my bum as annoyances. Now I'm more cautious, and try to always plan for a sharp exit if necessary.

Sexual violence in India is a serious problem, although to some extent you are safer as a foreigner, as men are more scared of the consequences if they go too far.

Staying in hotels outside of the capital calls for caution, however. I've lost track of the number of times someone

A woman walks past members of the Rapid Action Force in Bombay ©REUTERS/Savita Kirloskar
Note: Woman in photograph is not the author of this piece.

Protesters wave Egyptian flags during a protest in Tahrir Square. © REUTERS/Mohamed Abd El-Ghany

has knocked on my door after midnight, or even tried to get in. I always make sure the room has a decent lock, preferably a bolt, and have sometimes taken the phone off the hook to stop the pestering calls.

But with the annoyances come the advantages. There have been several times where I have been able to travel around tense areas in Pakistan less conspicuously than a male colleague as I can cover my hair, or even my face, and simply blend in.

And I may be wrong, but I think being a woman helps when you flash a smile at the border while sneaking into a closed country on a tourist visa after your journalist visa has been denied, as I've had to on three occasions.

On past undercover investigations, I've also felt people have been less suspicious of me because I'm female, and that offers a degree of protection and helps me get the story.

Since moving to South Asia, I've been more conscious of my gender than ever before in my life. Huge sectors of Indian and Pakistani society still hold deeply conservative views about the role of women, and often, as a westerner, I'm viewed as something of a third sex, an anomaly that nobody quite knows how to deal with, or what rules to apply.

This sometimes means I get access to both male and female perspectives in an otherwise divided society.

Has being a woman held me back in my work? I honestly don't think so. It can work both for or against you, and you have to take the highs with the lows.

In Pakistan men are often very respectful to women, which I know has helped with access to contacts or interviews – but you can also come across the odd misogynist, who prefers to talk to your male colleague, who happens to be your fixer.

The only time I can remember my boss being reluctant to send me on a story because I was a woman was when I was trying to track down the rapist of a British tourist in Rajasthan who had jumped bail. My editor finally conceded but only on the condition that I went with a male photographer.

I understood his caution, but generally you never want to make your gender an issue, or be seen to be soft, or be treated differently.

And why should you? My newspaper has a good safety culture, but I don't find many precautions taken are specifically gender-related. Nor do I believe they should be. Everyone faces universal dangers. Is it really more shocking if a woman faces violence, rather than a man? I don't think so.

A friend who was recently kidnapped in Libya pointed out that while she was groped, her male colleague was slammed on the head with a gun, and she questioned whether she had really been treated worse.

We do our jobs because we love what we do. As a woman you are sometimes in a weaker, sometimes in a stronger, position, and you have to adjust accordingly and sometimes take more precautions. But I never want my sex to define how I do my job and, honestly, I would rather just get on with it.

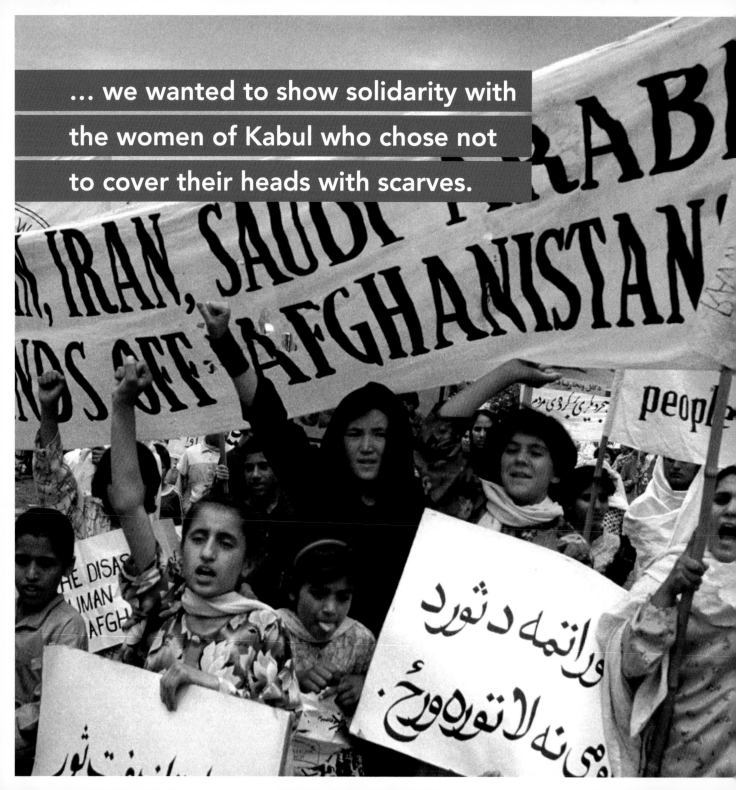

... we wanted to show solidarity with the women of Kabul who chose not to cover their heads with scarves.

jennifer griffin

DECEMBER 13, 2011. I am writing this essay while traveling with the Defense Secretary somewhere over the Indian Ocean en route to Afghanistan. We are about to touch down in Kabul and will fly by C130 transport plane to the border of Pakistan tomorrow – the same border where a group of US special operations forces called in an air strike on Pakistani forces in mid November throwing US-Pakistani relations into a tail spin.

My first trip to Kabul was in 1993 as a 23 year-old free-lance journalist. At that time the U.S. Embassy wouldn't allow its personnel or the Voice of America correspondent for whom I worked to travel to Afghanistan because it was too dangerous.

And it was.

The mujahideen were engaged in a 9-way civil war. There were no flights into Kabul, just a slow overland haul usually with the International Red Cross through the Khyber Pass past Jalalabad and Sarobi. I don't even know if Americans drive that road today. At the start of the war after 9/11, I recall one female Italian journalist and her two colleagues being pulled off the road and shot and killed by the river. It was not far from where nearly a decade earlier I remember a wild-eyed mujahid wearing women's sunglasses stopping the jingly bus that my husband Greg and I had decided somewhat foolishly to use to get back to Torkham Border. He asked for our passports and he easily could have pulled the two Westerners off the bus and left us by the side of the road. He didn't, but it was the closest that I felt I had come to being kidnapped. We were lucky. Many of our friends over the years were not.

In those days there was a debate among female journalists covering the Afghan war about whether or not to cover our heads. My colleague Kathy Gannon of AP

Members of the Revolutionary Afghan Women's Association chant slogans against the Taliban Islamic militia. ©REUTERS/Muzammil Pasha

L-R: An Afghan policeman tries to secure the area after suicide attack on a convoy of foreign troops in Kabul. © REUTERS/Ahmad Masood; Afghan women reporters set up their sound recorders in a media facility in Kabul. © REUTERS

and some Afghan women urged us not to, suggesting it would be hypocritical and a setback for local women who wanted to push back against the Islamists. The Taliban were just coming onto the scene and we wanted to show solidarity with the women of Kabul who chose not to cover their heads with scarves.

The decisions that we as female journalists covering wars make on a day-to-day basis are different than those of our male colleagues. These days I mostly travel with Pentagon officials on VIP trips so the journey is not that dangerous. From prior days and prior wars, the most important safety tip in my experience is to dress appropriately. No low cut blouses or sleeveless shirts. And literally cover your ass. Longer blousy

shirts or tunics are better than anything skin tight. Most of the convulsed countries are conservative, if not Muslim, and dress code matters. You don't want to invite unwanted attention.

Always have a local stringer from a strong family with prominence from the area of whichever trouble spot you land in. It should be someone of stature whose family is so respected that it would be considered a serious insult should you be kidnapped, robbed or harmed. This is the reason that I believe I was able to skirt through so many convulsed areas. I remember when we lived in Islamabad and had to travel through the Khyber Pass or en route to Pakistan's tribal areas to see the gun bazaar at Dera, we were under the protec-

Just because you can get away with something as a female journalist in these trouble spots, remember that one's actions can have consequences for the locals. They always pay a higher price. We can always leave.

tion of the prominent Pakistani journalist Rahimullah Yusufzai of the respected Yusufzai clan. Rahimullah later became one of the few journalists to have regular access to Usama Bin Laden as well as the Taliban. No one would dare touch you if you were the guest of Rahimullah and his sons. I even took my mom and two young sisters when they were 6 and 10 years old to the Khyber Pass in the back of a pickup truck provided by Rahimullah along with half a dozen armed guards.

In the Middle East, women journalists often have an advantage over their male counterparts because many of the male-dominated societies don't know quite what to make of Western women who aren't veiled. Sometimes women journalists can speak up and say and do things that their male counterparts can't. They can be pushier at border crossings and challenging the rules under authoritarian rulers or military regimes. I remember once sneaking out of my hotel room and escaping our Soviet holdover government minder in Kalmykia, a republic of Russia ruled by a maniacal dictator who likes to play chess. My colleague and friend Eve Conant and I sneaked out to meet one of Kalmykia's few dissidents, a woman by the name of Larissa Udina. I remember she made us cupcakes and spoke freely in her tiny post-Soviet apartment. Days later after our interview aired, Udina was taken from her apartment by armed government thugs, killed and thrown into a pond.

It was a wakeup call for a young reporter who had thought we had dared and outsmarted the doltish male minder for an interview that cost a woman her life. Sometimes just because you can get away with something as a female journalist in these trouble spots, remember that one's actions can have consequences for the locals. They always pay a higher price. We can always leave.

I remember in Somalia at the height of the famine in 1992 I was told by our local fixer Ali that we really should not wear any jewelry in public because the militias driving "technical" vehicles and high on khat could try to steal it. Weeks after Greg and I left Mogadishu, a cameraman for the AP was wearing a gold chain as they walked through a crowed market in the capital. Ali chased the young thug who ripped the chain off the cameraman's neck, only to be shot and killed.

I will admit that I never encountered any sexual assault while serving for 15 years overseas in many lawless and broken countries. I was lucky. Many of my female colleagues did. There were risks I took driving at midnight through Natal en route to an Inkatha conference when Mangosuthu Buthelezi challenged the ANC at the end of apartheid in South Africa. It turned out later that my escort, Themba Khoza, was Inkatha's main gunrunner. And the vehicle we were

driving was packed with AK-47s in the trunk. Had the South African authorities found us, it is not clear what would have happened. To this day I thank God that I never was physically assaulted. I put myself in far too many vulnerable situations as a young 20 something journalist, entering all-male migrant worker hostels at the height of the Zulu-Xhosa wars in the townships. Somehow I skated through.

December 15, 2011

After two days in Afghanistan traveling to U.S. military outposts we landed in Baghdad for a historic ceremony to end the Iraq War. It was pitiful in the fact that less than a handful of Iraqis showed up to pay their respects as U.S. forces were leaving. In fact the chairs set aside for Iraq's Prime Minister Nouri al Maliki and President Jalal Talabani sat empty with their names on the back and the number of the bunker that they should report to in case of incoming rounds. A pathetic statement as U.S. troops retreat. What struck me on the tarmac was how many female journalists were there to cover the end of the mission. In Vietnam it was a man's game – of course, there were the few pioneers. But as I looked around there were a lot of women journalists who either cut their teeth or made their name covering the Iraq war: Arwa Damon, Martha Raddatz, Joumana Karadsheh, Rebecca Santana, Jane Arraf, Barbara Starr. I was proud to be amongst these female warriors. The next day, however, Arwa Damon's cameraman was beaten up in Baghdad by government thugs.

Cairo and Tahrir Square was a turning point for women who cover the Middle East. The sexual assault of not just Lara Logan but also other female colleagues truly was a watershed moment in terms of risk calculations for female correspondents.

There is little one can do to eliminate the risks, but from now on when we take the risks to enter the fray to cover the march of history we will all be a little bit more on guard after what happened to our colleagues. Do we start carrying mace to the revolution? I don't know. But I do know it is a responsibility to be a woman in a war zone. Our negotiating skills often come in handy.

We can say things our male colleagues can't. We have access to more than double the population in conservative societies just by being women ourselves. And we can tell stories with greater empathy. The bottom line is we must keep going.

Jennifer Griffin *joined FOX News Channel (FNC) in July 1997 in Moscow. She was later assigned to the Jerusalem bureau in October 1999 as Middle East correspondent.*

She currently serves as Middle East Correspondent and is based at the Pentagon. She moved to Washington, DC, with her family in March 2007 after more than 15 years overseas working as a foreign correspondent.

As a documentary maker I have filmed in many situations where safety has been an issue...

janet harris

As a documentary maker I have filmed in many situations where safety has been an issue: as an embed with the British Army in 2003 and 2004, with the police, and during two series on homelessness made on the streets of London and Glasgow. Filming with a mostly male crew has its advantages, but I have often found myself alone and worried. It is frequently surmised that much of the danger to female journalists comes from groups of men, but the only time I have been physically attacked was by a group of bikini-clad prostitutes hurling hot tea and stones at me while I was doing research for a film on prostitution on the Reeperbahn in Germany.

This taught me a valuable lesson about camouflage and blending in. Sometimes this is impossible: for example, when I was an embed with the British Army in Iraq, the bright blue helmet and flak jacket tended to differentiate me from everyone else in the desert, before they realised I was even more out of place as a woman. But I have mostly found that it is being a journalist that sparks the most suspicion and hostility, rather than being a woman. If you are not welcome in a situation it is this added difference which can be used as a weapon, and there is little one can do except realise that discretion is the better part of valour and get away as quickly as possible.

When filming at the Jamiat police station in Basra in late 2004, when there were already signs that the militia were infiltrating the police, I found myself separated from the British soldiers we were filming. My first aid

A British Army soldier orders a photojournalist to leave the area while conducting a patrol in the southern Iraqi city of Basra. © REUTERS/Atef Hassan

...female programme-makers who work alone often have no female colleagues with whom to share experiences, and if they are not part of the foreign news pack, like myself, there are even fewer people to talk to.

pack and notebook were seized, and I thought I was going to be dragged off. My natural reaction was to smile and negotiate, which usually got me out of trouble – but I realised that it was my sex, not my profession, they were reacting to. I knew that I'd have to minimise this difference by acting more like a man and shouting for the crew, using my flak jacket to shove policemen out of the way. Groups of people smell fear – they quickly become pack-like, and in situations like that a woman is clearly not part of the pack. I stuck as close as possible to the biggest British soldier I could find and tried not think about what could have happened.

Another problem with being a woman in such situations is that I felt I could not be seen as a 'girl' in front of the male soldiers and crew and so could not show how upset I had been. Perhaps more importantly, I had no-one to talk to about the event afterwards. Soldiers can rationalise trauma by talking to their companions; female programme-makers who work alone often have no female colleagues with whom to share experiences, and if they are not part of the foreign news pack, like myself, there are even fewer people to talk to. A Nieman Foundation report at Harvard University (2009) has found that the majority of war reporters are single, and that female journalists are more likely to develop PTSD [Post Traumatic Stress Disorder]. I don't think the two are unconnected.

As societies get used to women in other roles, it might become easier to work as a female journalist. The adverse reaction [to me being a female journalist] from soldiers of the Royal Artillery, for example, who had women on the front line, was far less than when I filmed with the Black Watch, an infantry regiment who did not work with women.

Unfortunately being a journalist seems to be increasingly dangerous in many parts of the world, but as differences become smaller because of globalisation, television and social media, it becomes less acceptable for women journalists to be singled out because they are different from men.

Janet Harris *began her career at the BBC World Service for Africa, then moved into television, working for many years on BBC documentaries. She left the BBC in 2002 and worked as a freelance embedded documentary director in Iraq in 2003 and 2004 for a BBC documentary series on the British military in Iraq, and in Baghdad in 2003 and 2009 for independent television programmes. She is now completing a PhD at Cardiff University on the television coverage of the British military in Iraq from 2004 to 2009.*

I had to fight to get sent on my first assignment to Bosnia ... employers seemed reluctant to send women anywhere remotely dangerous.

anna averkiou

I had to really fight to get sent on my first assignment to Bosnia, at a time when some employers seemed reluctant to send women anywhere remotely dangerous. I've never felt unsafe because of my gender – the daily battle was dealing with sexual innuendo and discrimination from colleagues. But in the back of my mind I always thought that I didn't care what happened, as long as I wasn't sexually assaulted. I always tried to ensure that whatever I did was down to good practice and merit rather than playing on my femininity.

Towards the end of my first trip to Bosnia, my team received a radio message from a producer saying that an Italian APC [Armoured Personnel Carrier] had driven in to the back of one of our vehicles near the Red Cross building in the centre of Sarajevo. Immediately, the staff suspected the Italian IFOR [Implementation Force] soldiers – they were renowned for never giving compensation for accidents and local women often complained that they had no respect for them and treated them badly.

We pulled up at the scene to find our crew in the middle of a heated argument with a group of Bersaglieri,

and judging by the furious motion of the black capercaillie feathers on their helmets, the Italians weren't in an apologetic mood. As I clambered out of our vehicle – difficult when you're only 5ft tall and wearing the only available flak jacket in the bureau (which was extra large and down to my knees!) – they angrily wheeled around ready to do battle with the journalists' new boss – me!

I took a deep breath and prepared to enter the fray as I made the final step down onto the road. I turned, and as soon as they saw I was a woman, the feathered hel-

Sarajevo children play outside a building damaged by a tank shell. © REUTERS/Danilo Krstanovic

Thankfully, we were released unharmed – and it was only later, in the relative safety of Sarajevo, that I allowed myself to think about what might have happened....

mets came off, sunglasses were donned and combs quickly run back through hair.

"Ciao bella!" they greeted me with broad grins. I returned fire with my biggest smile, gestured at our smashed vehicle and shrugged: "Guys! What's happening?"

After much laughing, batting of eyelids and a coquettish attempt at Italian, I not only got them to agree to

sign and pay for the damage, but received an invitation to dinner at the officers' mess. Most importantly, I'd impressed the more chauvinist members of our bureau.

That same day – and in complete contrast – a cameraman and I found ourselves being forced out of Pale at gunpoint by Serbs, who were angry we'd been invited by the Organization for Security and Co-operation in Europe (OSCE) to film a prisoner

released unharmed – and it was only later, in the relative safety of Sarajevo, that I allowed myself to think about what might have happened...

exchange. Amid all the confusion and shouting, I decided not to argue with them. I put my hands up and did as we were told. Thankfully, we were

Anna Averkiou *is a journalist, news editor and trainer. She started her career as a reporter on local newspapers in North London before moving into television and working on documentaries for Channel Four.*

She went on to work as a producer and reporter with various national and international news organisations including Visnews (now Reuters TV), Worldwide Television News (now APTN), TV-am, Superchannel, MBC and BBC World News before joining the BBC's World Newsgathering Desk.

Anna now uses her experience and knowledge to help and advise clients on their media and communications strategy, with a particular interest in media crisis management.

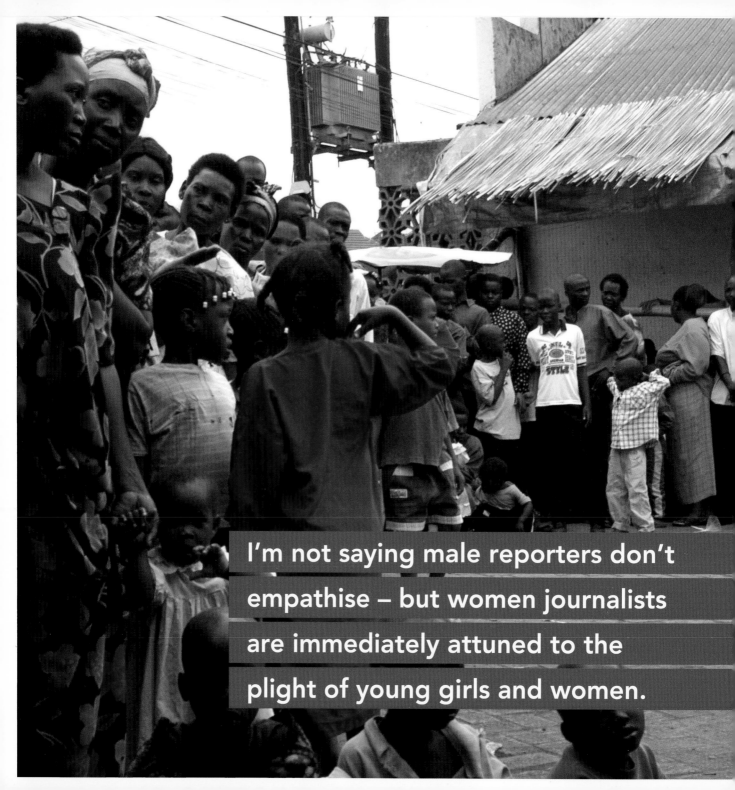

I'm not saying male reporters don't empathise – but women journalists are immediately attuned to the plight of young girls and women.

ann mcferran

It wasn't until I was in my late forties that I became really involved in writing about human rights and development issues. Whether it's in the UK or in Africa or India, human rights abuses significantly affect the lives of women and children. As a woman journalist you are drawn to their predicament and you want to make people aware of how appalling women and girls' lives can be in some parts of the world – simply because of their gender.

One of the first and for me, most heart-wrenching stories I wrote was for *The Times* magazine, in 1998 when AIDS was at its peak in Africa. I went to Kenya and Uganda where I saw that those who suffered most were the women: grandmothers, mothers and girls. The mothers because they had been infected, often fatally, by their philandering husbands; grandmothers because they were left to bring up many young grandchildren with little or no money. And I'll never forget meeting 10-year-old Mary, left to look after her siblings when her mother died of AIDS.

I'm not saying male reporters don't empathise – but I think instinctively, women journalists are immediately attuned to the plight of young girls and women.

Of course it would be ludicrous and pretentious to say that because you're a woman you understand what it's like to be a young Kenyan whose mother has died of AIDS and who has to look after five brothers and sisters with precious few resources; or that you have some immediate insight into what it's like to be a Darfuri or Rwandan woman who's been raped by the Janjaweed or the Interahamwe. But because you are a woman, girls and women will usually be open with you, and you will probably find that you achieve moments of empathy, and access to all-important personal detail.

For most of my foreign trips, including those to war zones like South Sudan and Darfur, I received very little safety training. I went to South Sudan with UNICEF

Ugandans wait in line for free voluntary HIV/AIDS tests in the Ugandan capital Kampala. © Reuters

and James Nesbitt, the actor, who was working as a UN ambassador, for a story on the rehabilitation of child soldiers who'd been forced to fight in Sudan's lengthy and brutal civil war. We had to get a UN certificate which was basically to say you'd been through some kind of safety training, which amounted to some slides and a bit of chat from a Sudanese UN guy. I certainly didn't find it remotely useful and there was no female focus to it. In 2008, I went to Sierra Leone, with David Beckham on his first trip as a UNICEF ambassador. I didn't have to go through this 'safety' training because I had the 'UN certificate'. I was told that Beckham and his retinue had to spend several hours in London, training for it, after which there was a lengthy exam. Frankly the greatest danger we faced wasn't from ex-rebels, but from Sierra Leoneans desperate to get Beckham's autograph or a glimpse of the great footballer. I'll never forget staying in a very basic hotel there, and the locals standing on each others' shoulders chanting Beckham's name as they tried

to see him eating his goat stew. It was the same with Robbie Williams, another UNICEF ambassador, during a trip to Sri Lanka in 1998. Tamils mobbing Robbie and pleading with him to adopt their children, were rather more overwhelming than any physical threat from the then civil war.

I've never 'done' war – because I'm more interested in the issues of post-conflict disaster, rather than the hurly burly of war itself.

I've felt very safe in most places, often because of the people I was with – often local NGO or UN people, other journalists and photographers. I'm not a particularly anxious or neurotic person, but I take natural precautions, for example I don't think it's very smart to walk around certain big African cities, like Nairobi and Johannesburg, by yourself. But I've worked in such places, with male colleagues and I felt safe with them, partly because they knew Africa and because they were guys.

But I was alone in Rwanda, in 2003, researching and writing a story on the women who'd survived the genocide, but been ignored by their own government and the international community, and were HIV positive. I always carried a mobile phone, which I think is essential wherever you were. And I found there that your local fixer – who's often both driver and translator and nearly always male can be a real ally.

I think women journalists should be treated the same as men. But in some Muslim countries, women need to be careful about the customs. You should wear baggy trousers or long skirts, cover your arms and consider covering your head. This is just showing respect. But you should also have confidence in your own abilities as a journalist, and there is no reason why being in a more male-dominated culture you should let yourself be bossed around.

In Uganda I wrote a story on child soldiers for the *Telegraph* magazine, with the photographer Marcus Bleasdale. We were heading from Gulu for Kitgum, a town just over the border from Sudan where children who'd been rescued from or fled the Lord's Liberation Army were rehabilitated. We hadn't gone far when we saw a vehicle at the side of the road, with two wounded men. Their vehicle was shot to pieces and two of the men were seriously wounded. Marcus was keen to talk to them, but our driver put his foot down. "I am responsible for you," he said, "We're not going any further. We are returning to Gulu." The following day we heard that one of the men had died from his injuries. The driver was right, and had made sure we were not in any danger.

The only time I've ever felt in fear for my life was in Darfur in 2005, and not because of the warring militias, but because of a thoroughly bad driver in a vehicle which shouldn't have been on any road, let alone one of the most dangerous roads in Darfur.

The aid agency I was with insisted, quite rightly, that we always drove in convoy and demanded everyone check in morning and evening by radio, before the nightly curfew. It was a dangerous time and I was trying to tell the story of the children of women raped by the Janjaweed militia.

Often we'd be driving to an internally displaced persons' camp and a UN driver would point to the bushes and say "that's where the Janjaweed are camping; only a few days ago x number of people were shot at and killed". One day, the vehicle I was in began to swerve, and the driver lost his place the convoy. We were alone on a notoriously dangerous part of the road where ambushes were common. The driver started to drive far too fast and zigzagging all over the road. I screamed, "Please slow down!" I thought 'I'm not going to be killed by some scary militia, but because of a bad driver in a malfunctioning vehicle.' But finally we got to the camp and did our interviews. I returned in a safer vehicle.

I don't think I've ever been in a situation where it's been too dangerous for me to get the full story. Don't do anything silly, of course but ask yourself "Why am I doing these stories?"

You may be surprised at your own answer but I feel you need to ask it! And it goes without saying you should then throw yourself into the story. For me these stories have been the most fulfilling work I've done, and I feel very privileged to have stepped into the lives of some people who are life's unsung heroes.

Ann McFerran *has been a journalist for forty years. She has written for The Sunday Times, The Times, the Telegraph, The Independent, the Guardian and Marie Claire, amongst others. Her investigation into how caste discrimination affected aid after the Gujarat earthquake, for The Sunday Times magazine, won Amnesty International's magazine journalist of the year award in 2003. She currently teaches on the MA Newspaper course at City University London.*

Try to fit in to the culture of the people you are doing a story on as much as you can.

fatuma noor

Being an investigative journalist and covering Somalia, one of the most troubled nations in the world, comes with its advantages and disadvantages. The advantage is that you could make a difference from the stories you cover – if not to a community, then to one person. This also comes with disadvantages, mainly because Somalia – with its own civil unrest – has not been easy to cover.

Somalia is mainly a Muslim country, and one that has been engulfed in chaos for more than twenty years. Islamic insurgents have continued fighting with the Transitional Federal Government, which has led to the loss of lives, among other problems. The Islamic insurgents have tried introducing the strict Shariah Law – something that is not accepted by the population. Women and children continue to suffer.

What's the most dangerous situation you have been in as a female journalist?

In 2008, I did an investigative report on a Somali brothel located in the heart of Nairobi. The owners of the brothel were located in Eastleigh (a location that is mainly populated by some Kenyans, and Somali refugees).

The owners of the brothel were bringing in refugee girls from the camps on the Somali-Kenya border, promising them a good job, but they were kept against their will. These girls were also below 18 – most of them were between 12 and 15, and could not speak any language other than Somali.

It was risky because the only way I could get the story was to go in as one of the refugee girls and 'work' as a sexual worker. Luckily nothing happened, but there

A Somali woman packs ginger roots in bags in the Eastleigh neighbourhood of Nairobi. © REUTERS/Thomas Mukoya

Photo to right: Somali women in veils walk along the main street in the Eastleigh neighbourhood of Nairobi. © REUTERS/Thomas Mukoya

were health risks involved. One of the girls who was rescued had HIV and others were pregnant.

I have also covered Islamic insurgents – mainly the recruits who were coming from western countries. I travelled with them from Nairobi to Somalia, but on our way there we were kidnapped. It was life-threatening because I was a woman travelling with men I was not related to, and working when they had banned working for women. After eight hours I was released with help from another person.

What experiences do you have of being based in cities or countries where cultural issues dictate that women are treated differently from men?

Coming from a very conservative community, it has not been easy [to work as a female journalist] – not only because of the community, but also because some family members have always had problems with my

career. I have covered the Somali community in Kenya and Somalia, where it is culturally wrong for a woman to ask men questions and to travel without having your husband or family around. All of these things come into play whenever you report on certain stories. My family continue to receive threats because of my job.

To what extent do you think being a woman has affected your experiences, either positively or negatively?

I have never tried to look at it from the viewpoint of a woman. Of course, there are some things I think would be easier for a man, rather than a woman, to do. Luckily, I have been fortunate enough to get all the stories I have researched. It has been very hard but I have always managed to get them. The brothel story could have been very hard for a man to do – so on this occasion being a woman worked for me. With the "Al Shabaab" story, being a woman worked for me because they trusted women more than they would men, but on the ground in Somalia being a woman worked against me because of cultural and religious issues.

What safety advice and tips can you offer female journalists based on your experiences – either positive or negative?

Try to fit in to the culture of the people you are doing a story on as much as you can. If I were covering a riot in a country such as Egypt, I would dress conservatively and have plenty of security when entering a crowd. Once a Kenyan journalist who was covering the Somali border was beaten because she wasn't dressed appropriately. Dress appropriately depending on the environment, and be aware of what is happening around you.

The second piece [of advice] would be to always try to have a plan B for every story you do. Anything might happen and you might need to get out of that situation. Tell people you trust where you are, where you will be, and who are you with.

Fatuma Noor, *a reporter with* The Star *newspaper in Kenya, specialises in investigative and feature reporting. Prior to this she worked as a reporter for Kenya National Agency and as a news correspondent for The Star. She won the Features Writer of the Year Award in 2010 from Radio Africa Limited and the runners up prize (Forum for the African Investigative Reporter) in 2009 for her story, 'Inside a Somali Brothel'. In 2011 she was named print journalist of the year and African journalist of the year in the CNN MultiChoice African Journalist 2011 Awards.*

Rioters have attacked me before simply because I am a symbol.

kate brooks

What's the most dangerous situation you have been in as a female journalist?

I think that civil unrest generally poses the greatest threat – mob scenes are very threatening and can become very violent very quickly. Rioters have attacked me before simply because I am a symbol. Diseases like typhoid pose a threat due to a lack of hygienic conditions. Being vaccinated provides some protection, but not total protection. Recognising signs of infection is important, and having a solid medical kit on hand is critical. Generally, in war the threat is in being collateral damage, rather than being targeted. Often risk cannot be avoided because being there is risky in itself. Having a good support team and war insurance are important too.

What experiences do you have of being based in cities or countries where cultural issues dictate that women are treated differently from men?

I've spent the last ten years covering the Muslim world from Pakistan to Morocco. Gender largely defines society across the region, but as a foreign woman I am generally treated like an honorary man.

How has being based in such locations affected the way you deal with issues of personal safety and health at home and at work?

Since I live in the region, "at home and at work" have often very much been the same thing. It's important to be respectful of local the culture and to try to blend in as much as possible.

To what extent do you think being a woman has affected your experiences, either positively or negatively?

Being a woman gives me access to the world of women, as well as men. I am frequently hired to tell women's stories in areas where men largely have no access. I don't feel that being a woman has really ever been a disadvantage.

To what extent do you think women journalists ought to be treated differently from their male colleagues?

They shouldn't be treated differently at all.

© ALLAN CULLISON

What advice and tips can you offer female journalists based on the experiences that you've had, as far as being safe or unsafe in your work?

I think learning some form of self-protection is vital. When riding in a car with a stranger, sitting directly in the seat behind the driver makes it easier to get out of the vehicle and harder for the driver to make a sexual pass. Sticking a sock in your underwear can help when people grope in crowds.

What do you think is missing in terms of the culture of safety for women in the news room or field from the perspective of your bosses or desks or colleagues?

I think first aid, self-protection and hostile environment training should be made more readily available to freelancers who are contributors or potential contributors.

What safety training, if any, have you received for your work? Has any of this had a female specific focus?

I personally sought out hostile environments training. In TV this is largely required by media organisations, but in print it's rarely addressed. The training was general, encompassing first aid, security issues and weapons. First aid courses should be done at least every two years.

Kate Brooks, *an American photojournalist, has covered the Middle East, Afghanistan, and Pakistan since September 11, 2001. Her work has appeared in* TIME, Newsweek, The New Yorker, The New York Times *and* Smithsonian. In the Light of Darkness: A Photographer's Journey After 9/11 *is her first book.*

anonymous

I have mixed feelings on how to approach the topic and I'm so tired of being seen as a gender – usually in a negative light – and not a person, a professional. I have a million things I could say that would be tips for anyone, but female-centric ones, less so. I work in a very male-dominated newsroom, and while most [of my male colleagues] are cool, a few aren't, and I just would rather not deal with their juvenile thoughts on the matter any more than I've already had to.

One armed guard was rather grabby with me in a car – his arm was around my shoulder and his hand reached down to my breast. I pushed his hand aside, firmly, but not violently, without looking at him (which I figured would challenge him – not a good idea. It seemed to do the trick.)

Hygiene-wise, I always travel with a toothbrush, Dettol [cleansing] wipes, a small towel and a few sanitary pads or tampons. In Syria, that came in handy because although I wasn't having my period, I said I was. I felt it might ward off the more rabid-looking guards, and so asked (very demurely) if I could have the pads from my suitcase. It worked. They left me alone.

I've heard about female correspondents being rather brash and loud around men in the Middle East, and that's never really a good idea, especially if you're in handcuffs and they're not. A little humility and respect goes a long way. I'm not saying bow down, but realise that in that moment, all of your ideas about equal rights don't even amount to a hill of beans when you're seated in front of a guy who might not grasp the notion of human rights – anyone's – to start with.

Wear strong, sturdy shoes. They give your presence and your movement weight, which, in many circumstances, can have the psychological effect of making

Your ideas about equal rights don't amount to a hill of beans when you're seated in front of a guy who might not grasp the notion of human rights.

you seem stronger to anyone who tries to mess with you. It sounds odd, I know, but I find it to be true.

In Muslim countries, they appreciate modesty – it's a virtue. If they look through your stuff and find a heap of makeup and colorful underwear (stuff that might be basic and ordinary to you might be seen as flamboyant to them), they might look at you in a way that you'd rather not be looked at, at that point. If you're going to such a place and think you might face an interrogation or investigation, it might also be worth making sure there are no party pictures of you online – drinking, or wearing things that authorities where you're going might frown upon. Believe me, the fact that there were no photos of me in bikinis online was helpful. My clothes were all black and modest. I had only a lip balm, eyeliner and a compact with me. They commented on this repeatedly.

As awful as the men in such places can be, they give themselves more of a license to hurt or violate a woman if they think she is already of 'loose morals' – your idea of 'liberated' might equal their 'Whore of Babylon'. Carry yourself with all the gravitas and dignity you can. This doesn't mean not crying or showing that you're upset (they'd find it unnatural if you weren't somewhat rattled). Rather, make their choice to harm you a major moral dilemma for them – even if you can't really understand their moral code. Having your period makes you unclean to most men in the Middle East, at least temporarily, and they'll leave you alone for that. Also problematic would be dishonoring what they consider an honorable woman. Speak of your family – your parents, your siblings, and ask them if they have sisters, daughters.

Opposite page: A riot policeman punches a Greek photojournalist during a demonstration in Athens on October 5, 2011. © REUTERS/Yannis Behrakis
Note: Journalist in photograph is not the author of this piece.

One editor wouldn't send me to Eritrea, saying he didn't believe women should go to war zones.

jenny matthews

I've been to quite a few dangerous places – El Salvador, Lebanon, West Bank, Chechnya, Afghanistan and Iraq – but it was always my choice. Unfortunately you can never predict things going wrong.

I have worked a lot in the Middle East and Afghanistan. There, women are treated differently, but this has nearly always been an advantage for me (although I still can't get the hang of keeping a scarf firmly in place) partly because most of my work has been about women and conflict. One picture editor wouldn't send me to Eritrea (even though I'd been there before, during the war), saying he didn't believe women should go to war zones.

I think things have changed: women [journalists] are now on the agenda whereas twenty years ago, unless there were sexy young women fighters involved, women hardly featured in reportage from war zones. I think Maggie O'Kane's reporting for the *Guardian* from former Yugoslavia set a bench mark for reporting daily life in a war zone – but still women are prepared to follow softer stories.

I think men and women should always be treated fairly, equally.

I have had safety training (SAS and Marines), although it was some time ago. I thought the first aid training was more useful than the kidnap scenarios. There was definitely not a female focus.

Opposite Page: Women stand in line for relief packs in northern Bangladesh. © Jenny Mathews/British Red Cross

TIPS:

- Do as much research as possible, talk to people who've been there, and don't feel embarrassed if you have to ask obvious questions.

- If you hire a fixer/translator/driver, make sure you've thought through the implications for them if things go wrong. If you are injured you can come back to the NHS, but they may have no security net.

- Road accidents are more likely than any other. Check who you are driving with, and don't be afraid to walk away from a dangerous driver.

- Always carry a torch , sweets, cigarettes (even if you don't smoke) something to buy you time if necessary.

- Dress practically , comfortably.

- Learn some basic words in the local language.

- Only pack what you can carry.

© LISA

Jenny Matthews *is a documentary photographer. She has worked all over the world for human rights and development organizations and her photography has been published in a wide range of magazines including* Marie Claire, Guardian Weekend, Sunday Times *and the* Independent. *Her book ' Women and War' was published in 2003 and she has exhibited that work internationally.*

ágnes rajacic

Virginity tests on women, harassment of foreign journalists in Egypt, group rape in Libya and Yemen. Although there was more equality after the Egyptian revolutions, remnants of the old regime spare neither men nor women. How should a foreign female journalist behave if caught up in the Arab Spring?

I still think I was saved by listening to the Egyptians. When we went to Tahrir during the revolution, it was not my first time in Egypt, and it was not my first time in the square. I had gone there in 2010 to do a series of interviews with young people – especially women. These energetic young people, whose desperate situation was unthinkable for a European of the same age, became my soul mates. I wanted to know about their future.

Entering the country
Unlike many journalists "parachuting" into Egypt, I was already connected to the country when the revolution erupted. While other journalists were busy looking for a safe hotel, my main concern was for the good health of my mates there. While waiting for my plane ticket in Budapest, I called up two friends of mine – Marianna, a young human rights activist, and Naglaa, a 35-year-old painter, for a briefing. Marianna, who

walked to the square every day, said to me : "In Tahrir we are safe – the revolutionaries are protecting us. You can come."

I am a freelance journalist and a consultant, and although I have received safety training, I do not have much security equipment or bodyguards. I wanted to travel with someone from the Egyptian community while in Egypt, to be on the safe side – but when I could not find another person to come with me, I had no choice but to go alone, counting on local support from the moment my plane landed. Fortunately, there was no mistake in this.

We organised the walks in shifts: One day I would go with Naglaa and his friends, and the other I would go with Abdelrahman, a young Egyptian working as a tourist guide downtown. It went without saying that we had to be cautious – putting a scarf on the shoul-

While this incident was not agreeable… I saw it as an unavoidable evil that one could face in any crowded European football stadium.

der and walking in between others were minimum precautions to take.

With my dark brown hair and somewhat Mediterranean features, many people in Europe think I could pass for an Arab. I thought that this, as well as my basic knowledge of Arabic, would help me out – as there was a growing paranoia against foreigners in Egypt. But once in Cairo, I realised that it didn't do the trick. No Egyptian doubted that I was a foreigner – in fact, I was thought to be an Israeli spy on two occasions, and was once confronted by a Hebrew-speaking Palestinian woman. My zero knowledge of Hebrew made me an unlikely foreign agent, and the suspicions were dropped.

The unexpected
Be aware of who you are with and where you go. The unexpected happened just when we thought the worst was over. On 11 February, a few minutes after the resignation of Mubarak, the ambiance was festive and we headed towards Tahrir. I was not afraid of walking around the square with my camera and dictaphone. My friends led me through the crowd and told me the "rules of the game" for women: If I wanted to speak to someone, I had to ask them first – an order that was, of course, almost impossible to comply with. Even so, I managed to speak to a dozen people.

Men behaved in a polite and friendly manner, and no one wanted to harm me in the slightest. But the air became heavy on the avenue leading from Tahrir Square to the 6th of October Bridge, where we had to walk between a military tank and a stage. Men and women gathered there to listen to Shadia's song, "My Love Egypt". In the middle of the crowd I suddenly felt hands on the intimate parts of my body – they grabbed me like spiders. I was paralyzed, but when I realised that this was not a one-off incident, and that many people wanted to touch me, I felt vulnerable and became angry. Instinctively, I wanted to smack the molesters – but they disappeared quickly. Touching and pulling went on for some minutes until people around me started noticing what was happening. My Egyptian friends closed the space around me and gave me precise instructions as they pulled me out: to finger-point at the people who were molesting me. They looked different from the bright, celebrating faces.

After taking me out of the crowd, my 'new bodyguards' turned against the attackers. An awful quarrel started. While this incident was not agreeable, I did not consider it to be a very serious case. Rather, I saw it as an unavoidable evil that one could face in any crowded European football stadium. I was more frightened to

Opposite page: A government supporter harasses a female journalist during confrontations with anti-government protesters in Sanaa January 29, 2011.
© REUTERS/Khaled Abdullah

L-R: A woman holds an Egyptian flag in front of riot police during a protest in Cairo. © REUTERS/Asmaa Waguih; Veiled Egyptian women run into a mosque to avoid teargas during clashes in Cairo. © REUTERS/Yannis Behrakis

learn that another more professional and certainly better equipped American reporter did not manage to come out of the situation as easily: Lara Logan had been reporting at the same time and the same place when she was beaten and seriously assaulted.

Was I lucky that, even as a suspected "Israeli spy", I had not been beaten up on 11 February? Was it my brown hair that protected me, even if it belongs to an obviously foreign face? Was I saved because I was not reporting for a well-known American channel, but only for the Hungarian media? Or because I was guided through the crowd by my Egyptian friends?
I believe that all of these elements helped keep me safe. I asked other Egyptian journalists about the incident, and they did not know any details about the perpetrators. While we were eager to know more about potential dangers facing female journalists, it seemed

that the Egyptian media was silent, and the international media reported these cases without looking for testimonies, or telling the slightest detail about the perpetrators. Instead, it talked about the "blossoming violence against women in Egyptian society", while ignoring the possibility of other elements and scenarios. It took an unbelievably long time for the western press to realise (if it did realise it at all) that the paranoiac autocratic power would not disappear from one day to another, and it would not treat foreign journalists with kid gloves.

The remnants of the power
The mixed intentions of the Egyptian military became clearer as the months progressed: Women protesters were subjected to virginity tests in the spring, violence broke out against the Coptic minority, and the November general elections were preceded by

bloodshed. That was when I came back to Egypt. After the deaths of more than forty protesters in Mohamed Mahmoud Street, it was not a big surprise to see that people fighting in the front line were being detained, harassed and beaten by the police. Naama Riad Hassan, a future woman candidate of the elections, warned that intimidation of women was a characteristic method of the old regime, and the Egyptian police had always used it as a tactic. I was stunned when I heard a French journalist was attacked in the square. Local opinions said the attackers were infiltrators paid by the old power. Unidentified thugs assaulting people and looting in the centre of Cairo were another danger to consider: Their tactics were to scare people with gunshots or explosives. When they scared about 200 people sitting in outside cafe bars, and picked up whatever was left behind, I had to run from them.

Yet these events did not discourage the presence of women on Tahrir. Even in the evening, nicely made up women arrived to the entrance of the square, which was fenced with a cord. The majority of them wore veils, but some of them came without. The women who frisked us at the entrance warned us: "Do not go to the left, we have seen some baltagijas" (the hooligans from the outskirts that sometimes infiltrated into the crowd). We made our way through the square, while several people asked out of curiosity: "Where are you from? What do you think about this situation now?" When the ring around us became too big, we had to move.

The situation for women has changed a lot since February 2011. Women went to fight, healed patients and organised fundraising. When fighting broke out on Mohamed Mahmoud Street many people were rescued when women built a life chain between the protesters and the police.

Women as well as men are targeted and killed by the remnants of the regime in Egypt. Without denying that the harassment of women journalists is a criminal offence in every circumstance, we should not believe that we are the exceptions.

Ágnes Rajacic, *a freelance journalist and consultant, has five years of experience in the media and specialises in EU immigration policy, civil society developments and intercultural dialogue in Maghreb countries. In 2011 she covered the Egyptian uprisings for various Hungarian newspapers and radio stations. She has been published in* Népszabadság *(Hungary's leading daily),* Magyar Narancs *(a Hungarian weekly),* La Clave *(a Spanish weekly) and* Al-Ahram *(an Egyptian daily), among others.*

The state of their vehicles, bullet marked and ripped, told the story of what happens if you get too close.

kate forbes

I'm at my desk in a new job as Africa producer for the BBC and above the water cooler across from me there is a small plaque. It is for Kate Peyton, who did this job before me. She was shot and killed in Somalia. I didn't know Kate, so it is not my story to tell. But it affected us all deeply. The trip had already been turned down by another producer in London. He felt it was too dangerous. Would Kate have been more likely to turn it down if she had been a man? If she had had less to prove?

In Eastern Libya, running the BBC's operation just before the NATO bombing raids started, I had little time to reflect on the tragedies and triumphs of women who have gone before me. But I did experience the same dilemmas. Most days we travelled to the front line. In the evenings we'd come back and tales of near misses would be shared with colleagues from other networks.

The state of their vehicles, bullet marked and ripped, told the story of what happens if you get too close.

But the decision to stay back, or ask my teams to move back when things felt particularly dangerous, seemed the most difficult decision to make.

It's easy to find yourself in competition on the ground, going ever further. But would putting ourselves in more 'near miss' situations really tell the whole story? Did it really have value editorially? We know war is dangerous. What is the rest of the story that we need to tell? Having the confidence to ask these questions, I think, will keep you, and particularly those who work for you, alive.

A rebel fighter fires towards a sniper from a hotel where foreign journalists are staying in Tripoli. © REUTERS/Zohra Bensemra

At one point one of our cameramen explained that, at his advanced age (40!) he didn't have anything to prove. And he wished that when he was younger, he had realised that. It was like I'd been given permission to stay. And permission to ask people to stay. That being the only woman on the team did not mean I had to prove I was braver and tougher and needed less sleep than everybody else. Those standards were in my head only. And it's those internal barriers, which are the hardest to break.

Kate had many reasons not to turn down the trip that became her last. But if her memory can make us ques-tion our own need to prove ourselves, then her mem-ory will keep us safe.

As a young field producer, I am very much the under-study to the brave women in this book. But I feel that above all, we must learn from each other. Look at what has happened to your colleagues. Ask their advice. A silly example – after Lara Logan's horrible experience in Egypt, I started wearing a sturdy belt. In the chaotic crush of an election rally in Goma, I was glad I did. Pulled backwards by a group of young men, I held tight to my equipment as I felt hands in my pockets, up my shirt, going for whatever they could find. I felt

But as the adrenaline ebbed, I knew it wasn't to do with being of the weaker sex. It was to do with the basic rule of riots. Never let yourself get in between the protesters, and the police.

attempts to get down my trousers and yelled out. The belt had given me valuable seconds, and prevented something really unpleasant. My colleague rushed to grab me. Such was the force of the crowd around me, it felt like being pulled out of rough seas.

Crowds and riots are always a challenge. During the anti-austerity riots in Greece, anarchists and policemen formed a formidable barrier. On the one side balaclavas and baseball bats, on the other batons and CS spray. Neither of them discriminates.

Anarchists hate journalists as they think they are organs of the state. Just next to me a photographer got too close. He was grabbed by a protester who used his camera to beat him viciously until his face was pulp. We were chased away from this gruesome spectacle with baseball bats. I found myself alone, trapped in between advancing lines of plastic-shielded riot police and a violent mob. Pushed and shoved, I lost my footing. As a bat swooshed past my ear I was grabbed by my shirt. A Greek journalist who worked for Mega dragged me back through the haze of tear gas and

planted me against a wall. 'This is no place for a girl like you' he said, as he walked away.

I felt annoyed and disillusioned. Maybe he was right. The material I'd got was good but like all things would be tomorrow's chip wrapper. But as the adrenaline ebbed, I knew it wasn't to do with being of the weaker sex. It was to do with the basic rule of riots. Never let yourself get in between the protesters, and the police.

I think, that with some thought about those who have gone before us, and some advice from those we admire, every place can be a place 'for a girl like you'. Or a girl like me. Every war zone, every disaster, every riot. We can tell the stories that need to be told, wherever they are.

Kate Forbes *is the BBC's senior producer for Africa based in Johannesburg. She works with the BBC's top correspondents, writes for BBC News online and recently led its deployment in eastern Libya during the war. She has also worked for Sky News and has had photos and writing published in national newspapers.*

What I have experienced so far is a sense of loneliness and powerlessness.

anonymous

I have worked for a national television station and I freelance for national newspapers and magazines. What I have experienced so far is a sense of loneliness and powerlessness. As a young woman I am often surrounded by old men (officials or senior co-workers) who look at me first as a young attractive woman and secondly as a professional.

If I am not alone on an assignment they will first speak to my male companion and later they will pay attention to me. Sometimes it is hard to cope with this situation. There is no female chief editor in national newspapers in my home country and only one on a television channel.

I have never experienced a threat to my personal security but I am very aware of the risks of sexual harassment (and take precautions). Once I experienced discrimination. There was a public demonstration in Rome and fear of riots. I was not chosen for the job and my boss explained: "We just want to protect you". But I quickly replied: "I would I have chosen another job if I wanted to be safe". Then they agreed to let me go.

One of the main safety concerns for female journalists is when they have to travel alone...

mon mon myat

Although some women, be they politicians, journalists or street vendors, might not feel comfortable being treated differently as a woman – in Burma, we're often regarded as the weaker sex and that means we are at risk.

Myat Su Mon, who works for the 7 Day Weekly News Journal, says one of the main safety concerns for female journalists is when they have to travel alone, especially after the recent murder of a female Japanese tourist.

She explained what happened on a journey with a motor bike taxi driver to a remote village in the delta in Burma.

She said the silence between her and the driver made her really nervous, especially when she realised they were the only people on the road.

"I tried to keep talking to the bike rider [about the fact] I'm a journalist and things related to my work, trying to make friends with him and build trust with him. Once his responses got friendlier, I was a little bit more relaxed".

However Mon held her breath until she reached her destination because she realised she was in a helpless situation if anything did happen.

In the remote villages of Burma where most women wear the traditional sarong, it is very rare to see women wearing less conservative clothes.

"I need to be very careful not to wear tight jeans or short skirts when I go to the villages. Otherwise it looks odd to the elderly people", Mon explained.

"But I wear loose jeans when I travel because it's good for safety and health", she added.

A woman looks out from inside a bus in Yangon. © REUTERS/Soe Zeya Tun

Journalist Eint Khaing Oo, 28, smiles as she awaits her release from Insein prison in Yangon. © REUTERS

Dressing like a model is not appropriate for female journalists too. Mon wears traditional dress when she goes for interviews with policy makers.

The editor from the 7 Day Weekly News Journal said increasing numbers of women were applying for reporter jobs in local publications, so more female journalists are being sent on field trips or to interview the government officials.

Tin Zar Zaw (34) from the Popular News Journal said "when interviewing officials, female journalists are better treated than male journalists".

But she suggested women should think about going with a male colleague.

"Government officials are very careful about accepting interviews conducted by a female journalist if she comes alone."

"I might be denied an interview unless I go with another fellow", she added.

In Burma, politicians, policy makers and businessmen often try to attract journalists by giving them a tip-off, which allows them the opportunity to use media as a propaganda tool.

Zaw suggested "the best thing a female journalist should do here is be ethical. Avoid doing husband hunting. Don't be so close with the sources".

Work for female journalists in Burma is poorly paid and unstable, with some women reporting they suffered stress and trauma in their work, which can often be dangerous. In a country where health insurance is a luxury to the journalists, it is often left to journalists to fend for themselves.

"I have to take care of my personal safety, but in some cases I asked my office to help solve the problems", Zaw said.

But sometimes it's impossible to stay safe. Eint Khaing Oo was arrested while she was taking photos of protesters in front of a United Nations office after Cyclone Nargis.

Oo says she was interrogated by the police in the jail and repeatedly asked insulting questions.

Finally she was sentenced to two years imprisonment for disrespecting the state.

"I don't want to remember the time when I was interrogated by the police especially their rude words and yelling to make me nervous".

Would this have happened were she male?

Mon Mon Myat *is a writer, photographer and journalist who has worked with IRIN News (a UN Office for the Coordination of Humanitarian Affairs service), AFP and IPS Asia Pacific, among others. She set up Creative Media House (CMH) in 1997, a media organisation which produces documentary films, books, features and news related to Burma.*

... safety was never an issue ... I've learned how to cope with situations.

patricia khoder

I was once covering a news story about a killing in a remote area of the Lebanese mountains. Two corpses had been found in an olive field only reachable by foot. Before leaving for the assignment, I did not change out of my dress or sandals, thinking it would be too late to see the bodies. I was wrong.

Once there, I wanted to find my way to the scene. I spotted a young man from the village who was guiding a group of male journalists. As I went to follow, he shouted at me, "You cannot go there, there might be snakes. The path is narrow, we have to climb rocks and walk through thick bush; you could hurt yourself." I looked at him with a surprised expression and said, "But you are wearing shorts and sandals, you will hurt yourself too." His response: "But I am a man."

I burst into laughter and followed the group.

I have been working as a journalist for fifteen years. I've covered riots, demonstrations, explosions, and political assassinations. For me, safety was never an issue. Yes, I did feel fragile and threatened but I've also learned how to cope with situations.

I started working at *L'Orient-Le Jour*, the oldest French daily in the Middle East, when Lebanon was still under Syrian occupation. In 1999, I was writing an article about censorship and wanted to interview a senior security official, who received me, but refused me the interview I was asking for.

I still remember his words, "You are here because I want you to deliver a message to your newspaper. We know how you all live at home; we know where you go and we know who you sleep with. Your newspaper has an excessive culture of freedom, you don't shut

Opposite page: A foreign journalist takes a picture during a rally marking Hezbollah's Martyrs Day in Beirut's suburbs. © REUTERS/ Mohamed Azakir

up. But we will teach you to do so. What do you think about that?"

I answered with youthful recklessness: "I think that we are living under a Stalinist regime." He said nothing in reply. I always wonder what would have happened then if I was a man.

A few years later, I was covering a political assassination. A young man affiliated with a Christian anti-Syrian opposition group was found dead. A police officer at the scene informed me the victim's personal belongings, (CDs, credit cards, a wallet) were still in the car, which I also observed for myself.

Later, while I was working on a follow-up to the story, I learned that the investigators told the victim's family his personal belongings were never found. I got in touch with the judge in charge of the investigation. While I made it clear I was just seeking out his opinion on this inconsistency in the story, he soon started calling me every day, threatening to interrogate me for hours alone in a room, adding that I might even be jailed if I didn't reveal my sources or change my version of the story. Following the instructions of the newspaper's lawyer, I went to see the judge instead of waiting for an arrest warrant. With a big smile and a timid-sounding voice, I convinced him I was so scared when I saw the crime scene, that my memory about the details had blurred.

In 2007 and 2008, I was involved in three separate incidents with Hezbollah militiamen. For some Lebanese, the Party of God is full of heroes, for others it is just a group of outlaws.

In October of 2007, a little over a year after the July War between Hezbollah and Israel, I was covering a story in a village in South Lebanon. Three men, dressed in plain clothes, approached me, identifying themselves as Hezbollah security members, and told me to leave the village immediately. I didn't. So they followed me.

Half an hour later, about a dozen men in civilian clothes and another six individuals on motorbikes, surrounded me. I told them that no one could force me to leave and that I was going to continue with my interviews. Since they couldn't argue with me anymore and because I am a woman, the men spoke to my driver instead. Talking about me as if I wasn't there, they said, "Let's have a man-to-man talk."

L-R: Lebanon's Hezbollah women supporters shout slogans during a rally in Beirut. © REUTERS/ Sharif Karim; A resident inspects a burnt car in Tripoli. © REUTERS/ Omar Ibrahim

That same year, I was with a Swedish journalist in Hezbollah's stronghold of Dahiyeh, a southern suburb of Beirut. A man on a motorbike soon approached us. Identifying himself as the Shia party's security officer he took my companion's passport and boasted, "You cannot do anything about it, the Lebanese police cannot interfere here." But I still called the authorities, and we spent four hours at a police station because I wanted to file a complaint against Hezbollah.

Scared or acting in cooperation with the party, they wanted me to change my version of the facts and file a complaint against an unknown offender. I wouldn't do it. Perhaps realizing the only way to get rid of me was to file the complaint, they finally proceeded.

Later that night, someone called from the station to inform me that the passport had been found. I went to pick it up, and again they pressed with more questions, and encouraged me to change the contents of the complaint. I spent another four hours at the station, repeating the same version of the incident.

In May 2008, Hezbollah militiamen took over Beirut for two weeks. The first day was marked by demonstrations. Road blocks were set up with flaming tires, garbage dumpsters had been pushed into the streets and sandbags were piled high along all the major roadways. While covering the story, I saw a group of about 30 people, most of them in balaclavas and kaffiyehs, throwing stones at someone. After noticing a piece of a camera – the zoom lens – in someone's hand, I realized the protestors had just attacked a photographer.

The only people in the street at this point were the rioters, members of the Lebanese army, and me with my notebook. When they saw me, they started running towards me shouting, "Journalist! Journalist!" I made a vain attempt to flee. Some men grabbed me by the hair, shoved me and continued to pull my hair while I fought back as best I could. They then grabbed a hold of my notebook and took off. All of this happened in plain view of Lebanese soldiers.

It took me three days to go out into the field again. The paper's editor didn't want me to work at that point, fearing for my safety. Disgusted, angry and scared, I needed to feel in control again; I needed to deal with my feelings and return to the field.

I've worked in the battlegrounds of South Lebanon and in the Palestinian camps of the country. I've covered wars and army withdrawals. I've been stuck in a minefield. But the risk is just the same for men as it is for women. So is that rush of adrenaline which makes you forget about the possibility of danger and pushes you to work even harder.

There have been times over these last fifteen years working as a journalist that I've acted provocatively or brashly with army and police officers. And a few times I've faced the reality that if I was a man I would have been arrested or suffer a worse fate.

I think in some ways, it is easier sometimes for a woman to report in the Middle East, so long as you can deal with the occasional condescending stare. As a woman, you are simply not taken as seriously as a man by people in charge – especially members of armed forces and militiamen.

At the same time, you always have to remember that when you are a woman working in the field or for the politics section of a publication, you must be extra careful not to make mistakes. In newsrooms, though they would never admit it, they always prefer to assign a man to what they consider a difficult task. Even if you've worked for years, one small error is enough to remind some editors that you are a woman, and that you "shouldn't be" in a war zone, let alone a newsroom.

Patricia Khoder is a senior reporter for L'Orient-Le-Jour, the only French daily in the Middle East. A Lebanese journalist, she has been with the paper for fifteen years. She has reported on the withdrawal of Israeli and Syrian troops from Lebanon and the assassination of Lebanese Prime Minister Rafic Hariri. She has also covered conflict in the Palestinian camps of Lebanon, explosions, sit-ins and riots in Beirut, and the Israeli war against Hezbollah in July 2006. Since the beginning of the Arab Spring she has reported on the refugee situation on the Lebanese-Syrian border.

samira ahmed

"Of course it would be much worse for the women." The ex-Royal Marine wasn't really trying to freak me out about rape. He was merely being honest with us journalists as we drove in the minibus back to the hotel, from our being-held-up-at-a-Bosnian-checkpoint-and-taken-hostage scenario.

It was autumn 1995 and the Hostile Environments safety course was still a relative novelty for my group of BBC correspondents, camera crews and producers. I could now patch up spilling intestines, identify the sound and range of certain artillery, watch for signs of a minefield, and whether a stranger was carrying a concealed gun. The scenarios may have changed since the aftermath of the Yugoslav civil war that dominated my first few years in the trade, but the principle training for war zones remains the same.

Safety in the field is still often thought of only through that dramatic and narrow perspective. As in news, the dramatic rare death makes the headlines. My experience as a young reporter on Northern Ireland covering an astonishing number of fatal road crashes helped me look out early on for the greater risks hiding behind the headline.

These are my key concerns based on my experience.

Hire the best vehicle and driver you can. Wear a seatbelt. Iran has some of the worst roads and most dangerous driving in the world. There are a lot more countries you could add to that list. The chances are you'll be spending hours on the road travelling between locations. I was all too aware on the pot-holed drive from Tehran to Qom, dressed in a chador, with no seat belt, nothing but quotes inscribed on the Quran on the roadside rocks to look at, that the odds of a violent death were probably higher right at that moment than at any other time in my life.

Watch out for idiots throwing things. It wasn't even a riot. It was a routine weekend in the marching season in Northern Ireland in 1996. I was standing behind a line of armoured police vans which were keeping angry Nationalist men out of sight of the Loyalist

Photographers and members of the media cover a gunfire at the Taj Hotel in Mumbai. © REUTERS/Desmond Boylan

march taking place behind us and out of sight of us. No Molotov cocktails. Just some rowdy shouting. The size of the rock that came flying over the barricade, and crashing a few feet from me was quite a surprise. It shouldn't have been. Being struck on the head by that would have been a particularly stupid death. I have a put a bit more thought into where I stand and awareness of what's going on around me since.

Enlist local help. I know this seems obvious, but it matters for more than your own individual safety. I worked with a local Sowetan born cameraman in South Africa to film a special report for Channel 4 News on so called "corrective" rape of lesbian women in some township nearby. His being big and tough looking, as well as streetwise, meant I could approach and 'vox pop' men on the street. They were astoundingly revealing about entrenched homophobic attitudes. But as a foreign journalist it also was important to have an honest local colleague to give their own reaction to what I was investigating. He admitted being shocked by what he was hearing in his own country; genuinely touched by the raw testimony of surivors of relatives that we interviewed. I could be satisfied, as we discussed each stage of filming, that our film was not prurient nor casually racist. It won the 2009 Stonewall Broadcast of the Year award.

In Iran in 2002, I was filming with an all-female documentary team (for Channel 4's Islam Unveiled), when two other British film crews were deported at the same time. Keeping focussed on responsibility was important. Even our crew was arrested for a few hours, but released without trouble. Sometimes exposing wrong-

doing means burning bridges. But too often I saw thoughtless Western journalists casually endanger local fixers by sexing up content. For the safety of our colleagues long term we owe it to each other to be responsible about what story we're really there to tell.

Samira Ahmed *is an award-winning freelance journalist and Visiting Professor of Journalism at Kingston University near London. She won the Stonewall Broadcast of the Year award in 2009 for her special Channel 4 News report on so-called "Corrective" rape in South Africa and made the acclaimed Channel 4 documentary series Islam Unveiled (2004). She presents news and arts programmes on BBC Radio 4, and writes on culture and politics for* The Guardian *and* The Spectator *arts blog. Previously a news anchor and correspondent at Channel 4 News (2000-2011) and at Deutsche Welle TV in Berlin (1998), she began her career as a BBC News trainee in 1990. She has been a reporter on Newsnight (1993-4) the Today programme (1995), and was the BBC's Los Angeles correspondent, covering the OJ Simpson case (1996-7). She is married with two children. Website: www.samiraahmed.co.uk*

It would simply be career suicide to admit any weakness or difference.

frances harrison

I have been detained, spied on, denounced on countless news bulletins and front pages, pinched, mobbed, screamed at by a wannabe suicide bomber in Iran, told off by turbaned bearded men for my 'bad hijab', prevented from asking questions in press conferences because of being a woman and even once hidden behind a curtain in a cubby hole in Swat in Northern Pakistan by a cleric who said he was on Jihad and therefore refused to speak with a female.

I've had my fair share of abusive and sexual phone calls, accusing me of giving blow jobs to terrorists and suggesting I should be locked up in a dungeon. Mostly I've been with camera crews or translators so I've rarely faced the physical dangers of being a lone female reporter in the field. But I've been kept awake by strange men knocking on hotel doors in wild-west towns full of men with guns or lain in bed wondering when I was going to be arrested. And it's not just me – my husband is a journalist who was shot in Kabul and didn't think to mention it till he got home, his hand in bandages.

There is a very male assumption that you have to be kidnapped or shot at to be affected by this job. It's a macho world where journalists are supposed to have just enough of an emotional response to the appalling suffering on display to deliver a compelling report, but no more. As a woman it's required to be even more stiff upper lip, more professional and even tougher than a man. It would simply be career suicide to admit any weakness or difference.

Strangely, by far the worst thing that happened to me was a court summons in Iran in 2006. I still find it very difficult to write about. It was the third summons. It arrived in the middle of one of those endless nuclear stories I covered as BBC Correspondent, which had me scrambling to be live on air on radio and TV every quarter of an hour. A courier brought the summons to the front door of our apartment block and I had to go and sign for it in person. I knew it spelled trouble when I saw the scales of justice on the headed note-paper but I couldn't read the document. Upstairs in

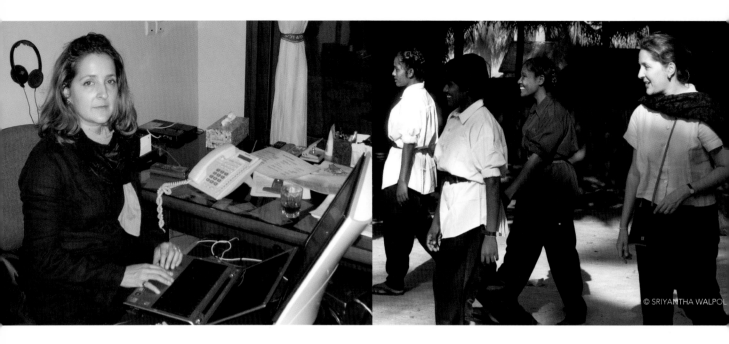

© SRIYANTHA WALPOL

the office my colleagues examined the summons with worried faces. They struggled to explain to me what it was about; finally I concluded it was incomprehensible legalese. All they could say was that I was the "criminally accused" and had three days to present myself to a revolutionary court in Tehran.

I should mention I was forced to work in Tehran on an Iranian passport because of being married to a British Iranian. The Ministry of Islamic Guidance had told me in no uncertain terms that if I wished to live with my son and husband, I had to enter the country as a local, which left me extremely vulnerable. I had no British consular protection as well as all the disadvantages of being a hated foreigner. It was a double whammy – the worst of both worlds. I was regularly branded "the enemy", with people chanting "death to the BBC!" at me and even once putting on a comedy routine ridiculing my reporting by broadcasting into a giant carrot instead of a microphone.

My court appearance had some comic aspects. My lawyer introduced himself to the unshaven scruffy judge by enumerating how many renowned journalists he'd represented, all of whom were languishing in jail. It was not a selling point as far as I was concerned. The first question the judge asked me was what was my religion – far from reassuring.

It turned out my accusers were estate agents, sharp men with slicked back hair and pointy shoes who wanted a hefty commission from the BBC for a flat

Only when I came back to London did I realise the toll taken by being constantly on edge, threatened and under surveillance.

they hadn't found us. They'd already threatened to attack our car that took my son to school daily, and I'd filed a complaint at the police station against them as a precautionary measure. In return they brought a criminal defamation case against me. It cost them the equivalent of one US dollar to file the case.

Waiting to go to court on an unspecified charge, I imagined the worst. Every morning I woke up at five o'clock, the anxiety eating at me from inside. I lay in bed rigid with fear, with visions of being separated from my child, whom I have still never told about this. Being a foreign journalist in Iran I knew any disgruntled individual could accuse me and then the case could easily escalate moving in unpredictable directions with my passport automatically seized, leaving me no way out of the country.

My fear was very real but the case happily turned out to be a damp squib and I moved on to the next story.

Only when I came back to London did I realise the toll taken by being constantly on edge, threatened and under surveillance. It has taken me a long time not to panic when a courier comes to the door or to admit, even to myself, that there were times when I was perhaps just a tiny little bit scared.

I badly needed a break but after all that adrenalin-infused reporting, doing a desk job in London was like

being suddenly buried alive. It resulted in my leaving the BBC after twenty years. My managers simply didn't understand that all that time in the field was catching up with me and being in an environment where it was unprofessional to admit weakness, I couldn't tell them clearly and unequivocally. Having spent their careers at desks they had no idea what it was really like to live and work in a permanently hostile environment – for them it was just a category on an insurance form.

But after Iran there were talks about whether the next post should be Kabul and I would point out its drawbacks for bringing up a seven year old child. I talked about a family friendly foreign posting in a place with good schools and they reasonably pointed out that this limited my options.

After working round the clock for years, I needed to spend time with my son who started suffering from panic attacks at school when he returned to England. We hadn't realised how much of the atmosphere of insecurity he'd absorbed as the small talk in our home was of friends being arrested and death threats. In London my unusual status as a "foreign correspondent mother" was treated as a bit of a taboo – something that couldn't be discussed openly for fear of being accused of discrimination or favouritism. I always felt it was something to hide, to the point that I ran around being tear gassed in street protests never letting on to the line managers that I was seven months pregnant.

Traditionally the foreign correspondent was young and male. Shockingly it was only in 1986 that the BBC appointed its first woman foreign correspondent. Since then most female correspondents have been honorary men – unmarried and/or childless – which is a high price to pay for an exciting career.

For every man in a conservative country who has discriminated against me for being a woman, there were ten more who warmed to me as a wife and mother. I became instantly less threatening and more approachable and in some ways more normal for them. It's easier to relate to people in conflicts and disasters struggling to protect their children if you too experience the primal urge to protect your offspring. Giving birth and nurturing a child's precious life puts a different gloss on dry casualty figures and it's hard to get so excited about sophisticated machines of death. Perhaps an awareness of human frailty kicks in that's a necessary balance to the self -image of the foreign correspondent as a hardened hack, unscathed by death and destruction.

Frances Harrison *read English at Trinity Hall, Cambridge and then did an MA in South Asian politics and economics at the School of Oriental & African Studies in London. She joined the BBC in 1989, working as a producer in TV and Radio in London and then was posted abroad in Pakistan, Bangladesh, Malaysia, Sri Lanka and Iran, and London as Religious Affairs Reporter. She won a scholarship to do an MBA at Imperial College and then did a stint working at Amnesty International as Head of News. As a visiting research fellow at Oxford University she has researched a book – the untold stories of survivors of the bloody denouement of the civil war in Sri Lanka.* Still Counting the Dead *will be published later this year by Portobello Books.*

zahera harb

Gender was never a question... I have worked as a broadcast journalist in Lebanon for more than 10 years, and have taken on many responsibilities within the news room – from being a field reporter, to editor, to news anchor, to current affairs programme producer and presenter. As a reporter I covered political, social and economic news stories, including several Israeli military escalations and operations against Lebanon, Arab foreign ministers' summits, Gulf leaders' summits, and international conferences. I was also assigned to cover the Prime Minister's official visits to several countries across Europe, the Arab World and The States.

Throughout those years, being a woman was not an obstacle. Each Arab country has its own distinct journalism culture and how female journalists are treated inside and outside the news room differs from one country to another. In the newsroom, I was the first to be asked to head to South Lebanon to lead the live coverage of the "Grapes of Wrath" Israeli operation against the Lebanese in 1996. I stayed 16 days in the south and built a base of contacts with local people – this helped us get first-hand information from villages we were unable to reach because of the Israeli bombing. The local people seemed to appreciate that I was a woman voicing their suffering on national TV. Some of them expressed their concern for the fact that I hadn't changed my clothes for 3 days and offered me clean clothes. They also offered us their houses to stay in after they knew that the team and I were sleeping in one of the local hospitals. I was never discriminated against, or attacked on the basis of gender.

I was sensitive to local customs, culture and traditions. I knew that when I had to cover a story in a conservative community, for example, I had to dress appropriately, without being told to do so. I had to approach people for information with the utmost respect and with the attitude that their help would be really appreciated. Did I gain access to information

because I'm a woman? I don't know – what I know is that, while pursuing stories, I was driven by my professionalism and not by my gender.

I haven't been in a hostile environment outside my home country, Lebanon. Hostile environments in Lebanon had mainly to do with internal clashes, or villages and cities being attacked by Israeli forces, and in both cases our movements and access to places were based on our knowledge of the local area. A local fixer is a must when you are covering stories in hostile environments outside of one's own country.

I have never received safety training during my work as a journalist and neither have my male colleagues, but I believe safety training is essential in situations of war and civil strife. I have had near death experiences, once during clashes between the Lebanese Army and some Palestinian factions in South Lebanon in the early 90s and several times during the coverage of the "Grapes of Wrath" operation in 1996. In both instances it was a matter of escaping bombs or flying bullets. This is where safety training is important. When you are in a battlefield, you tend not to appreciate the level of danger you are subject to and consequently you subject your team to.

At certain points, the story should not be more important than you and your team's safety. Holding a camera – which might be mistaken for a rocket launcher – meters away from an Israeli position is a

risk that might not be worth taking, if the image you are aiming for could be taken from a safer place with a different angle.

Zahera Harb is senior lecturer on the MA International Journalism program at the Department of Journalism, City University London. A former broadcast journalist in Lebanon working for Lebanese and international media organisations, she is the author of Channels of Resistance in Lebanon: Liberation Propaganda, Hezbollah and the Media (I.B.Tauris, 2011).

Opposite page: Relatives mourn the death of Lebanese youth Maher Hamad during his funeral in northern Lebanon. © REUTERS/Omar Ibarahim

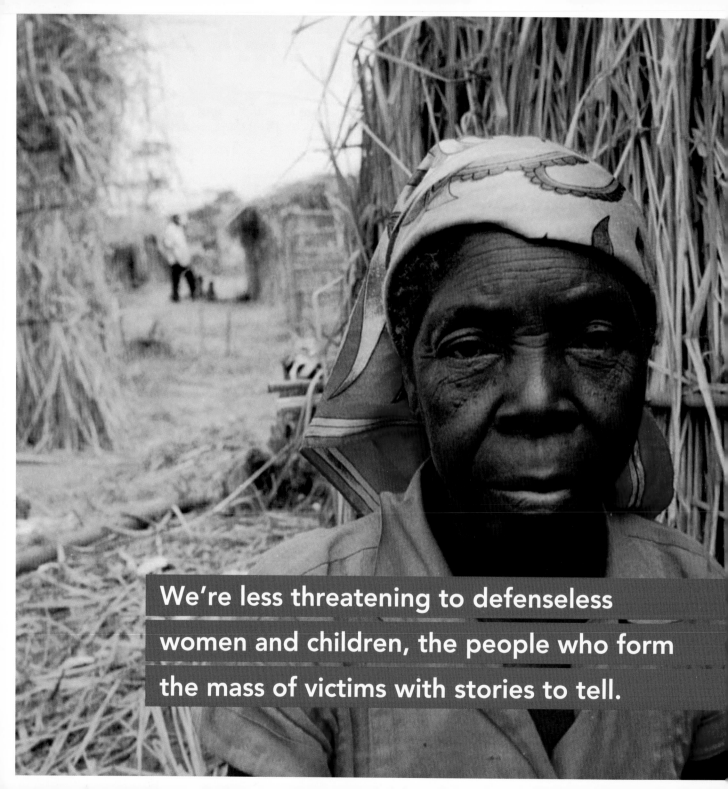

We're less threatening to defenseless women and children, the people who form the mass of victims with stories to tell.

judith matloff

The only time in my conflict reporting career that I received different treatment from the guys occurred in Johannesburg in 1993. Our Reuters bureau was finally – finally! – being outfitted with flak jackets to cover the violence surrounding the end of apartheid. Since a big part of the job involved driving into townships filled with men pointing assault rifles, I was very happy to receive body armor at long last.

What a surprise, though, when I opened the box. My flak jacket was red. The guys' were blue.

"That's because you're a girl," one of the cameramen joked. Everyone chortled. I left it at that.

Fortunately the gender distinction never extended to assignments. I was chosen to cover the worst tumult on the Durban coast. The civil wars in nearby Angola and Mozambique were my turf. My superiors routinely dispatched me at 4 in the morning to report on massacres. I worried about sexual assault, every woman who covers violence does, just as I feared being shot dead like some of my male colleagues had been. But if my bosses feared I would be raped, they didn't say.

Later in my career, I moved on to head the Africa bureau of *The Christian Science Monitor* and, again, no one questioned my ability to cover the nastiest of stories. Maybe it helped that I didn't report a narrowly avoided assault, or the sexual harassment that comes with the reporting territory. Sources and even colleagues made lewd advances, but I viewed this as an annoying part of the job. It happens in newsrooms, too.

I'm now wondering if our profession will change following the hideous attack on Lara Logan of CBS in 2011. I'd imagine that no managers would admit publicly that they would hamper a woman's chances at plum foreign assignments, but the desire to protect

Opposite page: A refugee from Angola's northern provinces awaits relief at the Caxito camp. © REUTERS/Mike Hutchings

© ROBERT NICKELSBERG © PHIL NELO

Indeed, instead of pulling women back from the field, managers should ensure they receive proper training in order to make sound judgments.

female staff may reign strong. So far it appears that female veterans of combat reporting are not being held back.

Let's hope they aren't. We ladies go into this line of work knowing the risks. The possibility of rape hangs over us, but so does losing our legs to landmines, as happened to photographer Joao Silva of The *New York Times*. To be honest, I'd rather be molested than unable to walk. And there's a case to be made that, as a general rule, women can navigate perilous terrain more safely than men. I've noticed that soldiers don't puff up with testosterone when women approach them. Army men often feel protective towards us and watch our backs more carefully, or

confess stuff that they might not to another macho. We're less threatening to defenseless women and children, the people who form the mass of victims with stories to tell.

Indeed, instead of pulling women back from the field, managers should ensure they receive proper training in order to make sound judgments. Employers should ensure rape prevention is introduced into safety training. Women must learn how to set verbal boundaries so that predators keep a distance. Women should hang alarms on their doorknobs so that predators can't break in. And supervisors should have frank conversations so that female staff feel comfortable confiding should the unmentionable occur.

© ROBERT NICKELSBERG

life. Blue was the color worn by the police so my male colleagues often faced hostility when they pulled up to barricades. But red? Who on earth wore a red flak jacket? It was a source of curiosity, if not amusement. I'm convinced that those gunmen wouldn't shoot someone wearing red, particularly when that some-one was a small, vulnerable-looking woman.

As a postscript to the flak jacket, it turned out that red served as an advantage. It might even have saved my

Judith Matloff *is North America Director of the International News Safety Institute, and she teaches a course about conflict coverage at the Columbia Graduate School of Journalism. A version of this essay appeared in* The Forward.

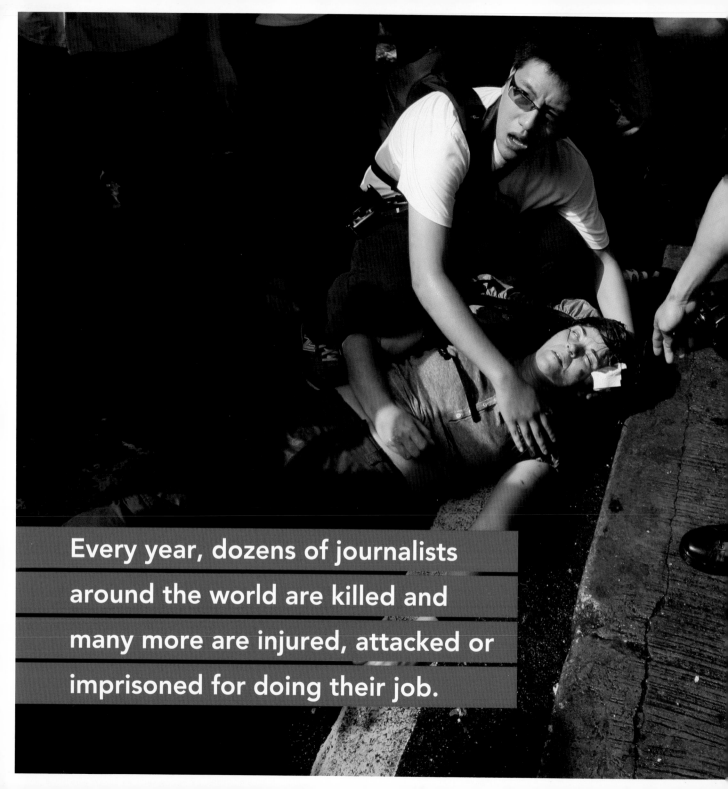

Every year, dozens of journalists around the world are killed and many more are injured, attacked or imprisoned for doing their job.

caroline drees

Every year, dozens of journalists around the world are killed and many more are injured, attacked or imprisoned for doing their job. Whether you're covering wars or an earthquake, protests or crime, journalists must work in fluid and often dangerous situations to cover the news. Women often face additional challenges, both at home and abroad. While there's no one-size-fits-all prescription for staying safe, the following guidelines and tips from women journalists may be a helpful start:

Be aware of your surroundings. This sounds so basic, but is vital. Do you stick out/blend in? Do you have an exit route? Where is the nearest hotel/police station/hospital etc?

Be aware of the culture in which you're operating, and adjust your behaviour accordingly. For example, in some cultures eye-contact can get you unwanted attention. In some, physical contact can be construed as an invitation.

If you're in a hostile environment, **try to make local allies**; find someone such as a village elder or anyone who is respected by local citizens who could help you if you get in a jam.

Beware of whom you trust. Sexual harassment is real, and can come from the people you suspect least. Don't assume you're safe with someone just because they are from your home country, or are officials, or seem helpful. Be careful where you go, and with whom – especially after dark. Try to use taxi drivers you know.

Opposite page: A man helps photographer Maria do Carmo Correia injured during a May Day demonstration in Macau. © REUTERS/Bobby Yip

"People's **perceptions of flirting are different**" in different places, a colleague advised. When interviewing people, maintain a formal/neutral style.

Try to **avoid travelling alone**.

Carry a telephone at all times, and make sure you have key numbers programmed inside. Also keep a printout of key numbers in your bag in case you lose your phone.

Consider carrying a second small, switched-off phone with you, if appropriate. On some occasions, journalists have to leave their phones at the door, and it can be a life saver to have a back-up for emergencies. If you do keep a second phone, make sure it also has all the important contact numbers programmed inside.

ID: carry some on you and keep copies of key forms of ID somewhere safe.

If you're part of a team, **coordinate with your colleagues** so everyone knows where everyone else is planning to be. "It sounds simple, but this can actually be really challenging in an environment where a lot is happening – a big protest, a gun battle etc, every member of a multi-media team is rushing to do his-her job in a different way," one colleague said.

If you're arrested, try your best to stay with a colleague and **avoid being separated**.

In countries where mace is illegal, try carrying hairspray in your bag. It's similarly effective.

Avoid speaking loudly in any language other than the local one, unless you want to focus attention on yourself.

If you don't speak the local language, try to work with someone who does. Among other things, this will help you gauge the mood of a crowd, understand if people are talking about you, and maybe help you leave a place before it gets ugly.

Avoid crowds; try to stay on the periphery, and always make sure you have identified exit routes.

Carry tissues for unexpected pit stops; a small bottle of hand sanitiser, wet-wipes and alcohol swabs are very handy; panty liners can be invaluable, especially if you don't get a chance to do laundry often.

Consider sanitary pads instead of tampons. In some countries, women having their period are such a taboo that an aggressor feeling the pad may be more inclined to leave you alone.

Also **pack a few Ziploc bags**; they're handy for stashing tissues/hygiene products, etc. in cases when you may not be able to dispose of them quickly.

Don't tell anyone you don't trust where you are staying.

The most frequent advice I hear from female colleagues concerns clothes, so I thought it would be worth including a separate section on dress sense:

"Overcompensate on clothes." "Dress appropriately for the situation/culture, and the same goes for local customs, gender rules etc." "I'd say the trickiest issue facing women journalists is harassment, be it verbal or physical… Appropriate attire is the biggest shield you can have." These are all bits of advice from female journalists.

Appropriate clothing "takes the focus off you as a woman and turns it back on you as a person or a journalist," one woman journalist said.

"In conservative … countries, ideas about women are often mixed, and include some not very positive stereotypes, and your clothing can play to them in an unhelpful way. What we consider modest can look sexy or at least attention-grabbing," said another.

"I generally wear trousers, a long top that covers the rear (this makes it more difficult for someone's hands to get access) and then I wear a satchel, over which (weather allowing) I wear a jacket or cardigan – it makes it more difficult for anyone to snatch your bag," one woman reporter advised.

Don't wear anything expensive or flashy unless you want to draw attention to yourself.

Scarves, scarves, scarves! Colleagues advised:

"(I keep) a scarf – for covering my head if necessary/keeping sand out of my face/keeping warm/cleaning up – in my bag. You can hopefully thus avoid the situation that a friend of mine found herself in this summer in Libya, when she ended up wearing a tablecloth. While we were told we were being taken to a political meeting (no head covering necessary), we were instead taken to a meeting of religious clerics – who insisted women could not cover the event without a head covering! Luckily a nice waiter found a … tablecloth she could use."

"I know of a female … journalist who was almost kicked out of covering a conference of President Robert Mugabe's ZANU-PF party because her skirt was deemed too short. Party officials only let her in after her colleagues scrambled to find a long sarong-style cloth for her to wrap around herself."

One Muslim colleague, who wears a headscarf (hijab), said police had grabbed her scarf and tied it around her neck several times to try to subdue her. For hostile environments, she recommended longer hood-style headscarves that can be tucked into your shirt or sweater and are harder for attackers to grab.

I hope this sampling of tips is helpful. Stay safe.

Caroline Drees is the General Manager of Middle East and Africa for Reuters. She has worked for Reuters as a reporter, editor and manager across the Middle East, Europe and the United States for more than 15 years. Named one of 150 women "who shake the world" by Newsweek magazine in 2011, she recently served as Middle East editor, Cairo bureau chief, and ran a UNDP/Reuters Foundation project to launch Iraq's first independent news agency.

Even when I know someone might want to hurt me, I always ask questions about family, about someone's children.

hala gorani

It may sound a little strange, but I'm most scared when I'm packing for a trip to a conflict zone. I become anxious when I have to think about what might go wrong. That's when I map out possible exit strategies if I do find myself in a tricky situation.

What if I'm detained? Can I trust the government minder who insists on taking our crew to a specific location? Is it a trap? What if I'm hemmed in by an angry group?

These shoes will allow me to run fast. This outfit will allow me to blend in. This headscarf will work for when I'm in a neighborhood where most women are veiled. Hide that hair when you must!

The past year has given female journalists no shortage of things to worry about: there are, of course, the threats that all reporters have to consider, but there are the additional concerns directly related to being female.

Many women correspondents who covered the Egyptian revolution were targeted specifically because of their gender. The nature of the attack was tailored to their sex. Lara Logan of CBS News was singled out, dragged off in a dense crowd and subjected to what her network called a "sustained" sexual assault.

Though my fears have never been directly related to what could happen to me as a woman, I've had a few close calls. In Cairo last year, a group of men surrounded me and shouted at me to leave. The day of the famous "camel charge" into Tahrir square, I had decided to spend some time on the pro-government side of the confrontation. I was suddenly pinned against the gate of the Egyptian Museum by several

Syrian refugee children stand on a road at the northern Lebanese border village of al-Mouqaibleh. © REUTERS/ Omar Ibrahim

Our driver, stunned by the attack, froze at the wheel. My screams to step on the gas pedal eventually got him going. The mob scattered and we made it out unscathed.

people, when a young man with a bandage across his face came to my rescue.

"Leave her alone, she's with me," he told the angry mob.

It was a man I had immediately befriended upon entering the hot zone a few minutes earlier. I'd spoken Arabic to him, had asked him what his name was. As a strategy, I find that this is one that has rarely failed me: show people you are friendly and open to listening to their story; speak their language. That man (whom I now believe was an off-duty police officer because of how deftly he extracted me from the crowd) wanted to help me because he saw me as a person in need, not a target.

Of course, none of that helped me the next day, when the car I was traveling in was surrounded by rock-

throwing thugs on a Cairo bridge. One stone shattered the window across from me and missed my head by a matter of millimeters. All the Arabic speaking in the world couldn't get me and my crew out of this mess. Our driver, stunned by the attack, froze at the wheel. My screams to step on the gas pedal eventually got him going. The mob scattered and we made it out unscathed.

Sometimes screaming and shouting works, I guess.

On a recent trip to Syria, I found that staying safe as a woman mainly meant trying to be as discreet as possible. In the same way men in war zones let their beards grow out, women know that the best policy is to cover up in certain neighborhoods.

But even when I am with those I don't trust, and even when I know someone might want to hurt me, I always ask questions about family, about someone's children. I think that coming from a woman, these questions create a connection. There aren't as many women as there are men working on conflict zone stories, even today, though our ranks have swollen. In the end, I want the people we are reporting on to feel we are human beings first and observers of a terrible situation second.

Of course there are the imponderables: roadside bombs, which I always feared while in Iraq; mortar attacks or sniper bullets. No amount of forward planning can help us then. Wrong place, wrong time. Bad luck. Those are the risks we take in the conflict zones we cover.

When I pack my suitcases for a trip to cover a story for which some of my colleagues have died, it is then that I think of the dangers. When I'm on the ground, the fears dissipate. I often ask myself if it's worth it. I always believe it is.

Hala Gorani *is an anchor and correspondent for CNN International and is based at the network's headquarters in Atlanta. She anchors the 1300ET/1900CET edition of 'International Desk' and often goes into the field to report on major breaking news stories. In late June she was part of a small team of journalists allowed into Syria for the first time since the protests began to cover the situation there. She previously reported extensively from Jordan and Egypt and has been instrumental in CNN's coverage of the "Arab Spring."*

Teargas canisters sizzling past, panic-stricken feet pounding, the crack of police gunfire, and then the coughing, spluttering impotence of rioters...

firle davies

I always wanted to be a journalist. My father was. And I wanted more than anything to be like him. When I left school I assumed that I would go to university and study 'journalism'. My father's response was swift and to the point; you don't study to be a journalist, you either are one or you aren't – go and get a job. I was eighteen when I got my first job as a sound assistant with Visnews covering what were then known as the Frontline States, north of apartheid South Africa.

I had a big boom microphone and headphones, and was attached to the cameraman by an umbilical cable. I quickly learned that I had to stay close, keep my eye on him, anticipate his next move, keep my sound levels steady and never, ever trip. I also learned the value of sound in television on the day I got my first hero-gram: a riot in the high density township of Chitungwiza. Teargas canisters sizzling past, panic-stricken feet pounding, the crack of police gunfire, and then the coughing, spluttering impotence of rioters brought to a halt – pictures and sound in perfect harmony, a great package for the evening news.

Television news was changing. For a start, it was too expensive. Cameras were changing. News was 24 hours. It had to be cheaper, faster, and everyone had to do more, be more if they wanted to survive. The term 'multi-skilled' crept into conversation.

I became a trainee cameraman in London, and had to learn even faster (I am still learning, by the way). It was brutal. A young girl in a very man's world. An old soundman colleague taught me a valuable lesson right at the beginning – when a programme editor asks you a question – always say yes. You speak Russian? Yes. Can you fly to Rwanda now? Yes, absolutely, no problem. Get your feet on the ground where the story is. You will soon know a lot more than anyone back in London. And then you had better make sure that you get the story right and first.

A woman displaced by war carries water through the rain at a makeshift camp near Goma in eastern Congo. © REUTERS/Finbarr O'Reilly

She wanted to see the people in front of her camera clearly. To sit down with them, to hear them speak, for as long as it took for them to tell, and try to understand, and not to have to leave when deadlines approached.

As an agency cameraman (woman) based in Africa through the 1990s, I worked alongside and against some of the greatest I have ever known. It was tough, physically – I still feel lopsided from lugging a great big camera on one shoulder, tripod on the other, a great rucksack of batteries, tapes and cables on my back, lifting silver flight cases off creaking carousels on to wobbly (usually broken) airport trolleys. I remember fumbling for re-importation documents, making sure the small US dollar notes were in the front pocket, and duty-free cigarettes easily seen as I made my way towards expectant-looking customs agents – who all had a habit, in the countries I frequented, of wearing

dark glasses no matter what time of day or night, and whose body language became positively drooling once trolley loads of silver flight cases started heading their way.

Those years were the crazy ones. When I look back on them now I can't remember the stories, just the thrill of rushing to an airport, speeding to a feed point, and the enormous satisfaction of seeing my pictures go out on the networks. The evenings spent with colleagues in beach bars drinking beers (oftentimes warm), trading war stories, dancing in local nightclubs to African rhythms that seemed to go on forever.

I never thought of the dangers and I am not sure that I thought very deeply about the people whose faces filled the frame of my camera, until a photographer friend turned to me one day, while we were stranded on a flight from Abuja to Lagos and all hell was breaking loose because the pilots were informing passen-

of camera, computer and satellite phone and broadcast from anywhere, anytime. I have a phone permanently attached to my ear, a crick in my neck, notebook perched, a pen in hand. I'm counting money, handing out money, writing receipts, having three conversations at once, sipping on water, puffing on a ciggie, slapping on sun block, organising food for the team, asking the driver to slow down, asking who wants a cup of tea, putting on a flak jacket, going to bed dirty, getting eaten by bedbugs, trying to find a place to pee, arranging vehicles, changing tyres, falling asleep in a room full of snoring soldiers, getting soaked in the rain, getting shot at, shelled at, sipping on a strong coffee that tastes like heaven, eating food out of a bag, playing Pink Floyd loudly on my iPod on a long road trip through the desert, having late night confidences with colleagues and friends, and early morning silences, sharing a whiskey at the end of a harrowing day, and always remembering the stories that we try to tell, and the men and women who tell them to us. It is a privilege. It is a lesson every day.

There are scars, but I wouldn't change them for the world. They are the people I met along the way, and the ones I lost too.

gers that we would have to divert to Kaduna, and quietly said that she wanted out. Out? Out, and that she wanted to see the people in front of her camera clearly. To sit down with them, to hear them speak, for as long as it took for them to tell, and try to understand, and not to have to leave when deadlines approached. That was 12 years ago. I thought she was nuts. That she was the very best in her business. That she would be leaving all this excitement and craziness, this immediacy of being there when something was happening. I have never forgotten her words. It has taken me a very long time to understand what she meant.

I work primarily as a producer now. And thankfully everything is smaller. I can get on a plane with a small bag

Firle Davies has worked as an Africa Producer for BBC News for 12 years, covering much of the continent including Zimbabwe, Sudan, Nigeria, Rwanda and Libya. Prior to that she worked for APTN (formerly WTN) as a cameraman and producer based in Nairobi, Kenya. She was named IWMF Elizabeth Neuffer MIT Fellow 2009/2010.

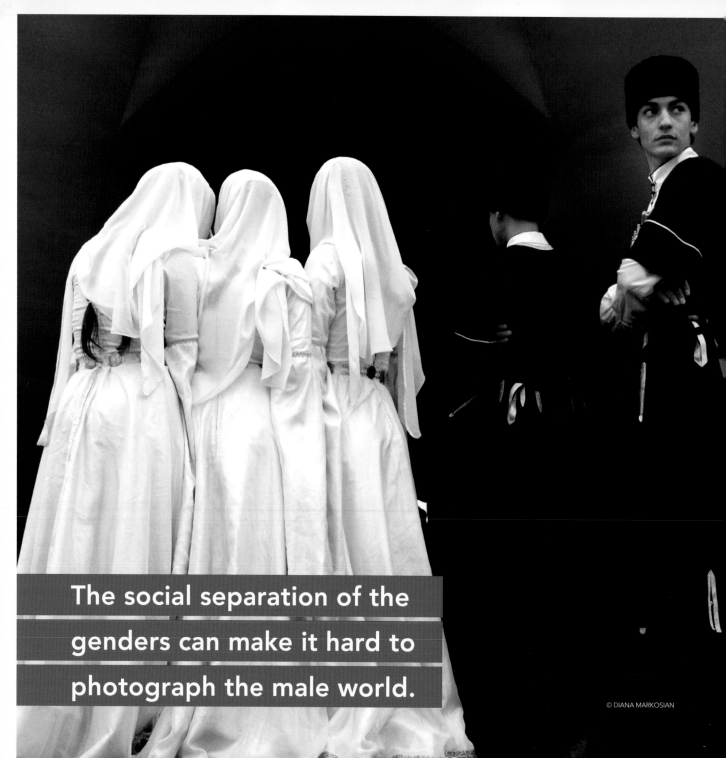

The social separation of the genders can make it hard to photograph the male world.

© DIANA MARKOSIAN

diana markosian

I don't think about it day to day. But if I reflect, being a woman covering the Caucasus is a big challenge.

I've made nine trips over the past year, to Chechnya, Ingushetia and Dagestan. My gender has always posed issues. It's not terrible, but attitudes towards women in this traditional Islamic society encumber access and mobility. A lot of male sources don't take female journalists seriously, and the social separation of the genders can make it hard to photograph the male world. For instance, I can't stay for prayers when photographing men at the mosque. Just getting permission to photograph them requires lengthy negotiations. Men in positions of slight power often like to use their authority to discourage me from reporting. I've had situations where guards or local politicians told me not to look into an issue or topic because "it's too dangerous and no place for a woman." It was initially incredibly difficult to understand this mentality, especially growing up in America with a single mother.

Daily reporting poses some of the biggest challenges. It starts in the morning when you take local transportation. People are constantly trying to put females down. A man in Ingushetia commented on the fact that I sat beside a driver of a mini bus. He asked me, "Aren't you ashamed or embarrassed." He followed with, "What do you think your husband will think at home?" There's little room and respect as a woman and even less as a female journalist. In downtown Grozny, the Chechen capital, you can't walk even a block at night without a constant stream of men curb crawling. They roll down the windows and make lewd comments. The harassment makes me think twice about report-

PHOTOS © DIANA MARKOSIAN

ing after dark, even though the city has become quite safe in terms of violence or crime.

I've had big problems in Central Asia, too. My least favorite place to work was Tajikistan. I could not walk around during the day without feeling uncomfortable. Men would stare at women like they were hunted prey. Sometimes I went home during the day just to get away from the public harassment. It made me feel dirty, even though I did nothing to attract unsavory attention. I dressed and behaved appropriately. But as a woman in these places you're vulnerable, no matter what you do.

Diana Markosian *was born in Moscow and emigrated to the United States as a child. She now works as a documentary photographer in Russia and the former Soviet Union. Her work has been published in* The New York Times, Boston Globe, Bloomberg Markets, Wall Street Journal, Reuters, *and* Human Rights Watch. *Markosian holds a masters degree from Columbia Graduate School of Journalism.*

adriana gómez licón

I have never considered myself in danger of being sexually assaulted or attacked because of being a woman. At worst, I have covered the slums of Ciudad Juárez where you get a lot of comments from men in the street. I have also visited dangerous places in northern Mexico and bad neighborhoods in Acapulco – a hot spot in Mexico's Drug War.

Freelance journalist Judith Torrea says that she has written stories that were critical of the army and the government. A campaign was launched against her because of this and she was called names.

More recently, two female journalists were killed in Mexico City. They were left naked in a park. It is not known if they were sexually assaulted. It is also not clear whether or not they were killed for being journalists.

I have felt in danger while covering stories, but I don't think I felt in danger because of my sex. Once, I visited a rough neighborhood in Ciudad Juárez an hour before two shootings happened and seven people were killed. I also learned later that a hit man had been killed there just hours before my visit – but I was unaware of the dire situation at the time. While I was there, some teenagers were looking out from the rooftops and asking me questions – who I was, and who I was reporting for. I told them I was a reporter and then ignored them. My team and I left straight after that.

There was another time when I was driving my car near to where a shooting had taken place in a soccer field, killing seven – mostly teenagers. A white van stopped in front of me on a dirt road, not letting me drive on for what felt like an hour (but was actually three minutes). I did not honk my horn, or do anything, and I waited for another car to come by to drive around the van. I was terrified.

I have felt in danger while covering stories, but I don't think I felt in danger because of my sex.

At military checkpoints, soldiers have been very nice to me – but they have said things like, "why is a lady covering these kind of stories?"

I have spoken Judith Matloff, a journalist and Director of INSI North America, about how I feel editors have sometimes stopped me from covering stories just because I am a young woman and could be in danger, instead of making it safe for me to go – for example, they could send a photographer along with me, or allow me to hire a stringer. At the time I was working as a reporter for the El Paso Times. El Paso, Texas is right across the border from Juárez. It is an easy drive, but sometimes I'd rather go with a photographer or a stringer. My editors did not give me that option, so I had to take the dangerous route by myself to cover my stories. It was the only way.

Adriana Gómez Licón *worked as a staff reporter for* El Paso Times *before becoming a correspondent for* The Associated Press *in Mexico. Her stories mainly cover 'narcos' (drug trafficking) , immigration and politics.*

A little girl holds onto a tape used by the police to cordon off a crime scene near the site where several people had been shot dead the night before in Ciudad Juarez. © REUTERS/Jose Luis Gonzalez

... **Russia is at the top of the list of the countries with the largest level of crimes against women journalists.**

galina sidorova

No Matter What

Last November I conducted a seminar for students interested in investigative journalism at the Moscow State University School of Journalism. Thirteen students attended, among them two gentlemen and eleven ladies.

And that is very characteristic of the profession nowadays. Journalism in Russia – especially 'field journalism' and investigative journalism – has become a female job. The reason is simple: it is low-paid and dangerous. According to information from the International Federation of Journalists (IFJ), Russia is at the top of the list of the countries with the largest level of crimes against women journalists.

The paradox is that Russia remains a male-dominated society in many ways – and the attitude to professionally successful women is often inadequate. I have experienced this more than once in the course of my long journalistic career.

When I started (at the end of the "good old Soviet times"), I happened to be the only female correspondent at the *Novoje Vremya* news magazine. They didn't treat me seriously – they just thought I was going to marry one of my well-established colleagues, and that's it! So, I had to work twice as hard, and be twice as smart, to move on. My advice to colleagues confronting similar problems is to ignore any mudslingers and to work hard. You will win in the end.

And now – a few words about the 'dark side' of being a woman journalist. This is something we do not often talk about publicly.

Besides being professionals, all of us are still women and, so, adorable and attractive. I had a really confusing experience at a ministerial summit devoted to the unification of Germany – I was a special correspondent with *Novoje Vremya* and covered most of these important meetings at the end of the 80s. I interviewed one of the high-ranking participants one on one – I don't want to release his name, since he is still alive, although retired – when suddenly he rushed up to me and tried to kiss me. To say I was embarrassed is to say nothing. I was so shocked that I... burst out laughing. The irony helped to cool him down, and finally I somehow finished the interview. I never told my editor what happened. I had to interview this guy more than once – he never made another try. Advice to fellow sufferers – just laugh and you will get a chance to take control of the situation!

The next case is of different origin. It occurred during my first trip to Kabul in the beginning of the 90s with a small group of journalists covering negotiations on the Russian Prisoners of War (POWs). We talked with Afghan diplomats, and I was so absorbed in conversation that I somehow missed the moment when our hosts suggested that we should go back to the bus. The situation in Kabul after the Russian (Soviet) troops left was unpredictable – different Islamic groups fought for power, not only in government institutions but in the streets. I happened to be the only woman in our journalist gang, and my male colleagues in every way showed concern about my safety – but not that time. I only noticed that I was alone with Afghan experts – who spoke quite good English – when I felt the natural desire to visit the ladies' room. I looked around for our interpreter but he had also disappeared. What was worse was that at the same time I realized that I was on male territory – no women worked in the building and so they only had men's rooms, crowded by smoking local diplomats. Since I physically could not wait any more I thanked everybody for the interesting discussion, muttered something about having to join my colleagues (whom I had no idea where to find) and

then, plucking up my courage and leaving my shame behind, I addressed one of the guys who somehow seemed more 'European' to me. I told him that I had another very important visit to pay before I left the ministry, and that was to the lady's room.

He hesitated, but nevertheless led me to one of the premises drowning in smoke and crowded by men. They all stared at me with unfriendly interest while he led me to the toilet cubicle, and I later realised he left me there, so I had to find my way back through this agitated crowed all on my own. Thankfully I was dressed in a long-sleeved, high buttoned blouse, jacket and pants.

The third case is the most difficult case, because it cannot be settled by laughter, irony or pretending to be cool. There is one thing that makes a woman journalist absolutely vulnerable.

It happened two years ago when I was the editor-in-chief of *Sovershenno Secretno* – an independent Russian newspapers specialising in investigative journalism. I got a phone call from "a friend". The voice on the phone sounded polite and silky – it advised me not to publish a story on corruption in a big Russian company in the defense industry: "Think of your children – they are still young!" the voice said.

My husband died of cancer eight years ago. My kids are still young. But the newspaper still came out with this story on the front page because I knew the moment I showed weakness they would crush me and crush the newspaper. And I cried.

And I still have no advice for that. You just do it no matter what, or you don't.

Galina Sidorova *is the Chairperson of the Board of Founders, at the Foundation for Investigative Journalism. From 2001 to 2010 she was the Editor-in-Chief of* Sovershenno Secretno, *the first independent Russian newspaper specialising in investigative reporting, and won the Artiom Borovik award in 2007. She has been a staff writer, an analyst, a special correspondent with the Russian weekly* Novoye Vremia, *a political advisor to the first Foreign Minister of Russia, and in 2010 was elected Vice-Chairperson of the Executive board of the International Press Institute.*

Staying below the radar is a useful skill ... Working in Islamic countries is a particular issue which has been much discussed among women journalists.

tira shubart

Working as a journalist in some of the more interesting places and sometimes alarming places around the globe, I don't feel that being a woman has to carry more risk than being a man. It's fairly risky for everyone nowadays as we know too well. Nor does being a journalist carry more risk than being one of the people who live in the places we cover who don't a choice to jump on a flight and head into or out of trouble. That said, being aware of specific local risks and cultural perceptions is absolutely vital for all of us.

Staying below the radar is a useful skill. And this often means dressing in an unobtrusive and practical way for women – until Harry Potter's Invisibility Cloak is on offer to all of us. Working in Islamic countries is a particular issue which has been much discussed among women journalists. Having covered Iran regularly for over a decade, I had many opportunities to think and sometimes moan about wearing Islamic dress. Yes, I found it irritating at times and very hot at other times. And until I developed a keen sense about the posi-tioning of my scarf, I did find myself sometimes being ticked off by the Pasdaran – Revolutionary Guards.

I soon realised that if I had several ropush made for me in Tehran – the Islamic covering worn by middle class Iranian women – and bought my scarves and shoes at the bazaar, I could blend in. It helped having dark hair – this is a lot harder to do if you are blonde and blue eyed. But armed with semi-decent Farsi and local clothes, I was able to get around Tehran even when

Opposite page: Women walking through market in Tehran. © REUTERS/Ahmed Jadallah

© DOM LEVER

the minders from the Ministry of Islamic Guidance prevented male colleagues from leaving the hotel during one period in the Iran-Iraq War. Of course this is trickier if you are carrying cameras and microphones, but dressing in local clothes does make life easier. In the back of a local taxi, nobody took any notice as I drove around southern Tehran looking for the neighbourhoods which had been hit by Iraqi Scud missiles. This was true on many occasions.

Working in other places – Somalia comes to mind – no amount of dressing up is going to help most women blend in. But wearing clothes that cover up and make one a bit shapeless is useful. Tight, revealing or sleeve-less clothes are only going to make everything more difficult and attract attention.

On one trip in Somalia, my camera operator – the delightful Anna Roberts – and I discovered that Somali women have a great degree of flexibility as regards clan affiliation. Which allows them to function as peacemakers and traders and a level of respect is accorded to them by the men – who are all identified by their clan. Consequently Anna and I were able to turn up in situations with male Somali warriors and get exclusive footage on a number of occasions. There were other times when it was simply scary for anyone; getting caught in a fire fight in a market and a minefield.

The biggest advantage to being a woman comes with access. In Somalia we were able to film an extraordinary meeting of woman who were setting up roadblocks in an attempt to stop fighting in one area. No men were allowed to film their meeting, but they were hugely welcoming to Anna and I and we were the only journalists there. In Iran, countless times I have been welcomed into family quarters with the women and children – as well as the more formal social occasions when foreign women were accorded a welcome due to long traditions of hospitality. The men were only able to get half the story.

Many women have had these same experiences in covering stories; there is still a certain novelty to women in the field. And I have no worries about taking advantage of this, up to a point. If a smile and some charm works to gain access or get an interview, that just leaves more time for simply doing our job: finding out what is happening and telling the tale.

Tira Shubart *is London based and has worked in 40 plus countries including extensive work in the Middle East, Africa, the former Soviet Union, Eastern Europe & Central America for the BBC, CBC, Frontline TV News, Monitor TV, ABC and NBC London bureau. Tira was one of the six founders of The Rory Peck Trust and remains a trustee. She also writes comedy about journalism and her BBC2 series "Taking the Flak" was based on her work covering African conflicts and filmed in Tanzania.*

Our job as journalists carries with it an inherent risk ... because we go to places and events that people are trying to get away from...

zeina awad

Our job as journalists carries with it an inherent risk that affects us all, irrespective of our gender or ethnic background, because we go to places and events that people are trying to get away from: disaster zones, violent confrontations, and unrest. However the way that that risk plays itself out can be gender-specific.

In the field, being a woman can disarm aggressiveness and defuse tension in interactions with authorities who have the power to facilitate or block access and passage. That same 'female factor' can also spiral out of control and turn into a threat of sexual assault. We heard horrific stories of female journalists of different nationalities being attacked during the Egyptian revolution in 2011. There are many other cases we have not heard about because the victims are not western. They don't have the same access and publicity; they may not be as comfortable talking openly about an issue that's considered private and sensitive in some cultures, or they may worry that any frank discussion could portray them as weak and incapable of braving the dangers of field journalism.

The sexualization of women at the expense of their intellectual capacities is a wider social dynamic that can creep into the media field as well. For instance, it is one thing to have male interviewees be extra attentive to a female journalist; it is another for that female journalist to experience a cloud of unwanted and uncomfortable sexual energy hanging above what should be a professional interaction. It is one thing for a conservative man to act modestly around a female journalist, it is another for him to treat her as if she is a

Opposite page: A supporter of Egypt's former president Hosni Mubarak (C) tries to run as she is attacked by anti-Mubarak protesters outside the police academy where Mubarak's trial was taking place. © REUTERS/Mohamed Abd El-Ghany

sexual temptress who belongs in the private sphere of a home, and not the professional world.

Within media organisations, female journalists have made huge strides, and are regularly given breaks – in my experience, some of the most supportive bosses I have had have been men. It is common in today's world for women in their 30s to be executive producers, correspondents and photographers. It is hard for me to imagine that there was a time – when these same 30-something year old women were still children – when men dominated those jobs. But women still have to deal with issues from that bygone era, like the pressure on female reporters and anchors to maintain their good looks. Unlike men, most women are not allowed to age gracefully on screen. Women can also find themselves navigating a rigid culture of male bonding from which they are excluded. After-hours meetings over a drink or private conversations with superiors are spaces where access to decision-makers is established, and interpersonal relations are developed. This is not something you can put your finger on, it may not even be conscious; rather, the culture of male bonding is rooted in unspoken beliefs about who should be included in the decision-making process, and assumptions about which gender has more worthy ideas and contributions to make.

I consider myself lucky to work with and learn from some talented men and women, and to be in a profession that feeds my boundless curiosity about the world and allows me to bear witness to incredible and at times heart-breaking events – from the war on Gaza, to tens of thousands occupying Wall Street in New York, to elections in Lebanon, to the ravages of poverty and disease in India and Sub-Saharan Africa,

to refugees stranded in the middle of nowhere on the Iraqi border, in the depth of the Algerian Sahara, and in no man's land between South Africa and Zimbabwe. I have met and been humbled by wonderful people along the way; unlike international journalists who come and go, they are people who are stuck in difficult situations because of fate or circumstance.

Throughout all my experiences I have often found myself being the only woman on the team and I consistently receive a great deal of support from my co-workers. Male producers keep an extra protective eye out for me while reporting from locations known for a high incidence of sexual assault; a colleague once

My hope is that as a journalistic community, we are able to cross into the territory of an honest conversation about issues affecting female journalists in the field and within media organisations.

insisted on giving me his flak jacket in the middle of an unexpected street battle while we waited for more to be sent to the scene. My hope is that as a journalistic community, we are able to cross into the territory of an honest conversation about issues affecting female journalists in the field and within media organisations. This is not about different treatment for anyone; this is about discussing things that we have only just started exploring. It is factually wrong to say that these dynamics do not exist – one only needs to look at how many female journalists were attacked in Egypt to see recent and graphic evidence that they do.

Equally I don't think we're served by turning the discussion into a narrative of female victimisation. As such, I believe that our dynamic and ever-evolving journalistic culture is served better by engaging with these issues in a way that's constructive for everyone – female journalists and fellow male colleagues alike.

Zeina Awad is an Al Jazeera English correspondent. She's been based in London, Doha, and Washington DC, and has covered the Middle East, Africa, and the Americas for news and current affairs. A globe trotter with a passion for stories and an addiction to news and documentaries, she's reported from many countries, including Palestine, Israel, Lebanon, Syria, Morocco, South Africa, Kenya, India, the United States, and Canada. She is currently reporting for Fault Lines, AJE's flagship Americas current affairs programme. You can follow her on Twitter @zeina_awad and Facebook Aljazeera Zeina Awad.

...one of the biggest failings of media organisations is that they assign journalists to cover dangerous stories without adequate training...

elia baltazar

Before the Mexican government launched its offensive against drug traffickers, female journalists here were confined to covering "social" issues, like culture or politics: areas which were traditionally considered "suitable" for their gender.

Only a few managed to break into stories about the police, security or justice, and even fewer were involved in covering issues like drug-trafficking.

But the violence that has spread throughout our country has changed that.

Female journalists in Mexico, who consist of the majority of the country's editorial staff (with women reporters making up an estimated 60 percent of the workforce), face the same threats as their male colleagues. But they also face additional risks in their work.

There is a lack of safety information for women who are dedicated to covering dangerous stories.

In Mexico, just one organisation has attempted to document the conditions of women in the media. In 2008, Comunicación e Información de la Mujer (CIMAC), carried out a study into the "working conditions of women journalists", which highlighted the disadvantages they face at every level of the profession. It is the only organisation to document attacks against women journalists, of which in 2011, there were 28 reported cases.

Among these were four murders – a number previously unheard of in the history of attacks against female journalists. And the violence is getting worse.

Maria Elizabeth Macias, editor-in-chief of the daily Primera Hora, in Nuevo Laredo, in the northern state

Opposite page: People stand behind the bullet-riddled window of a restaurant in Mexico. © REUTERS

of Tamaulipas, was found decapitated, with a warning message left beside her body. She was a journalist and ran a blog which exposed and condemned acts of organised crime.

The same happened to Yolanda Ordaz de la Cruz, a reporter for the daily Notiver in Veracruz, whose body was found beheaded and abandoned behind the newspaper's offices.

Women are also murdered because of their gender. This happened to Marcela Yarce, who worked in magazine advertising, and Rocio González, a business-woman and Televisa reporter.

Additionally, three female journalists, Lydia Cacho, Olga Wornat and Anabel Hernandez, have had to receive protection from the authorities because of death threats: Lydia, because of her investigations into cases of child molestation involving businessmen and politicians; Olga, because of her investigations into drug trafficking, and Anabel, apparently because of her investigations into political powers in Mexico.

But one of the most heartfelt cases was the disappearance of María Esther Aguilar in 2009, a reporter from Michoacán – she is the first and only female journalist about whose disappearance nothing is known.

And then there are the journalists who left their jobs after being threatened; this happened to Karla Tinoco in Durango and Ángeles Mariscal in Chiapas.

The list also includes cases of physical aggression, sexual threats, harassment and the authorities confiscating equipment. In the majority of these cases, though, a lack of confidence in the judicial system means complaints aren't filed and impunity reigns.

Journalists who share their experiences say that one of the biggest failings of media organisations is that they assign journalists to cover dangerous stories without adequate training, and without ensuring their safety.

Every day, greater numbers of female journalists end up covering violence in dangerous areas. These women, in some cases, have to resort to training themselves in order to ensure their safety.

But the majority have found themselves working in dangerous situations without any security protocols and without any job benefits to compensate for the danger. The situation for female correspondents in outlying states is worse still, as almost all work as freelancers for national newspapers, in exchange for a basic pay of 4-8 dollars for a published piece, depending on the publication.

There is absolutely no job security for them, despite the risks they face while covering subjects like people trafficking, security and migration, to name a few. The best salary these local reporters can expect is around 300 to 400 dollars a month.

However, more and more women are being recognised for the work they do – such as Marcela Turati, a reporter for the weekly *Proceso* and author of the book *Fuego Cruzado* (Cross Fire). The *Diario* newspaper in Juarez also has a team of women journalists, and their work has been recognised by international awards.

But these examples are exceptions to the rule, because a lack of guaranteed safety continues to be the norm for female journalists in Mexico.

Alongside our work as journalists, a number of us women have launched an organisation dedicated to improving journalism training and standards, solidarity amongst male and female journalists, and the condemnation of acts of violence against the press in Mexico. And we've worked to build bridges between journalists and civil society organisations in a bid to protect freedom of expression. This is the work that we've achieved since the launch of *Periodistas de a Pie* (Grassroots Journalists' Network), the organisation that I belong to and in which we – women, reporters and academics alike – work together, driven by the need to defend journalism and promote its quality, ethics and safe practice.

Because of *Periodistas de a Pie*, we have come to value once again our profession, the solidarity that exists between female colleagues and the profound commitment we have as journalists to prioritise people and the defence of human rights.

– *Translated by Hannah Storm*

Elia Baltazar has been a journalist for 23 years. She has extensive experience of working in the media. As well as collaborating with various websites and magazines such as CNN Mexico, Expansión, Día Siete, Animal Político, Open and Playboy, she has taken on the role of reporter, editor and managing editor at several national newspapers including La Jornada, El Independiente and Excelsior. She co-founded "Periodistas de a Pie", a grassroots journalism network, and has worked on a number of international publications concerning issues in journalism, including Harvard University's Nieman Reports. She currently produces and hosts Ponte en Medio on radio Código DF.

But in traditional societies, where hospitality trumps ideology, we are almost always accorded the special privileges afforded to guests.

lyse doucet

No Man's Land: Reflections on a working life as a third gender...

There is a question I get asked a lot: "Isn't it really difficult for you, as a woman, working where you do?"

For most of 30 years, working mainly across the Middle East, South Asia, and Africa, I have answered no.

But in recent years, in some places, it's become more difficult, and sometimes more dangerous.

Maybe I've just been lucky.

But in most places I've worked, Western women have been regarded almost as a third gender. We aren't treated like the women of the place. We aren't treated like the men. But in traditional societies, where hospitality trumps ideology, we are almost always accorded the special privileges afforded to guests. In conservative societies, that also includes a belief that women need to be protected.

I remember the acts of kindness. There was the man in 1984 at a crowded bus terminal in Abidjan, Ivory Coast, who approached me as night fell, and risk rose, to ensure I knew which bus I was taking.

There were the two Mujahedeen fighters in 1991 who gripped my hands as we strode, as quickly as we could, through a fast running stream in eastern Afghanistan to escape Soviet helicopter gunships tracking our movements.

And there are the many Egyptian men last November who linked their arms, and encircled me, and my two female colleagues in Cairo's Tahrir Square to escort us through rowdy crowds late at night.

The much publicised sexual assault in February last year in Tahrir Square on the broadcaster Lara Logan – and her courage in reporting it – helped put this issue of sexual harassment and safety on the agenda in a much more significant way.

It made western female journalists working in the Square more cautious. Egyptian women, who've dealt

In more than twenty years of working in Afghanistan I can count on one hand the number of times where being a woman posed a problem. In all of them, a solution was found.

with harassment for years, already knew the risks. My Egyptian colleague Shaimaa Khalil, who wears a head-scarf, says it doesn't matter how you are dressed and who you are; you can still be a target.

Women journalists have started looking out for each other. Last week, on Twitter, an Egyptian friend Yasmine Rashidi sent this message: "Leaving maspero. For female tweeps heading here be alert – sexual harassment galore."

But this isn't new. In some conservative societies, where contact of any kind between men and women is restricted by cultural and religious mores, we learned very quickly to avoid large mainly male crowds. In Pakistan in 1988, I told a visiting Canadian colleague she should avoid wading into the boisterous election rallies unless she was flanked by her male colleagues. She ignored my advice, perhaps thinking it was sexist or believing she couldn't do her job unless she was in the midst of the action. She was so badly groped she had to return to the hotel.

In early 2011, in Tahrir Square during the extraordinary protests, I was fortunate in being able to go in on a daily basis with an Egyptian who worked with us as a driver and producer who had experience in close protection work. He instinctively stood behind me everywhere we went in the crowds such that Egyptians

started recognising him from our TV reports. As it was, the mood and spirit of Tahrir in those first heady weeks of the revolution was, for all women, unusually safe.

What has become more of an issue is the rise of Islamist groups with a stricter interpretation of their religion. That can translate into minor gestures like not shaking hands, or more challenging ones like insisting they won't do interviews with women. I have had many occasions where men won't shake hands – from fighters in Libya during the 2011 war, to Iran where it's official policy. Fortunately I have never had to deal with a suggestion that a male journalist should be sent instead. (And my editor says he wouldn't accept that condition.)

But even this possibility can be exploited for all the wrong reasons. A feisty American friend working for a major American TV network during the US led invasion of Afghanistan was told by her desk in late 2001 that a male colleague was being sent to replace her because they couldn't send a woman into southern cities like Kandahar. There's nothing like being more Taliban than the Taliban.

In more than twenty years of working in Afghanistan I can count on one hand the number of times where being a woman posed a problem. In all of them, a solution was found.

In 2001, when I was told by colleagues that an Afghan Taliban leader in Pakistan would not see me because I worked for the BBC, and was female, I saw it a test of my belief in Afghan hospitality. I managed to politely make my way into his offices in Islamabad and extended traditional greetings. After a brief flicker of surprise, and a smile, he immediately opened his door to me, and an interview – my theory was proven right, so far.

A decade earlier, the forces of the prominent Mujahadeen commander Jalaluddin Haqqani – whose network is now on the US terrorist watch list – had taken the strategic city of Khost. I called his office to ask to accompany him and his men when they travelled to the area which was coming under retaliatory fire. I was told the BBC was welcome but women were

not. Searching for a compromise, I quickly offered to dress like a local man with my hair tucked up in the traditional Afghan flat cap. The suggestion was accepted without too much fuss. Then, a few days later, at a news conference at their headquarters in the Pakistani tribal area of North Waziristan, I was given the chair next to Jalaluddin Haqqani – dressed like an Afghan man, but with the privileges of a western woman guest.

I still don't know if his son Sirajuddin, now said to be behind most of the attacks on Kabul, would accept an interview with a female journalist. He is mostly in hiding, on the run.

But as long running conflicts intensify, and new ones emerge, the dangers are mounting.

We used to think militant groups would tend not to kidnap women journalists (or aid workers or tourists) but that reassurance has been shattered in recent years. In 2004, the kidnapping and killing in Iraq of the widely respected Irish aid worker Margaret Hassan felt like a defining moment. She had lived and worked in the country for many years, and had married an Iraqi. Some of us asked then: who is safe?

On more day to day issues, there's that question of what to wear which is not just about fashion. When I lived in Pakistan in the early 90's, we often discussed the value of wearing the shalwar kameez, the long tunic and loose trousers worn by Pakistani women. I, like many Western women, wore it. Its one of the few places I've worked where women do adopt the local apparel. Its comfortable, fashionable, and cool in the heat. My own view is that if it also helps me to do my job, in a respectful way, I have no issue with it. Some colleagues refused to wear it, insisting they preferred their normal attire ie jeans and shirts. At that time, in the 80s, we tended to say western women should wear what they felt most comfortable in. A woman walking awkwardly in someone else's clothes seemed to only add to her vulnerability. But as the culture in Pakistan, and many other places, has become increasingly conservative, I think that's changed this assessment. But women must make their own choices about what feels right for them.

At the opposite end are cultures where sexual relations can be regarded as natural as eating or drinking. In West Africa, in the 80s, I was sometimes asked straight out whether I "want to do it." A polite no was enough to deal with it – in most cases.

A few years ago, when a younger colleague told me she was heading to West Africa, I hesitated but then let her know she may have to contend with sexual approaches. I then regretted saying it, wondering if she would think I was being a bit prim. Weeks later, when she returned from her trip, she thanked me for the advice with a laugh. She ended up inventing an husband, and buying a cheap wedding ring, to fend off all the advances.

I have to say that I tend to see these risks and challenges as part of the job, not something that means women need to be given special attention, or worse, stopped from going anywhere. Sexual assaults can also happen to men, as well as women. But I don't think women can just dismiss some of the specific risks for women.

My own view, which has stood me in good stead, is that in many situations one of the best weapons is good manners, as well as a suitable dose of humour rooted in an understanding of how its used in the country where you find yourself. There should be no compromise on asking the questions that need to be asked, but there are different ways to ask them, and different ways to show respect for the country and people you're with.

Working with a colleague from the country, who knows the language and culture, is another crucial safeguard. That and an experienced team – whether it includes men or women – can make all the difference to one's sense of self and safety on the road. The more you know about the place, the safer you are.

For male and female journalists, the most serious threats of being kidnapped in some places, or shot at in others, are not gender specific. And they are, sadly, on the rise, and of course not just for journalists.

We are all safer for understanding all the risks so we can all work together, and support each other, to tell the stories that must be told.

Lyse Doucet *is an award winning Senior Presenter and Correspondent for BBC World News TV and BBC World Service radio who is often deployed to anchor special news coverage from the field and report across the BBC including Newsnight.*

She played a key role in the BBC's coverage of the "Arab Spring " across the Middle East and North Africa. She is a regular visitor to Afghanistan and Pakistan from where she has been reporting for the past two decades.

Her work has also focused on major natural disasters including the Indian Ocean tsunami, and more recently Pakistan floods.

Before joining the BBC's team of presenters in 1999, Lyse spent 15 years as a BBC foreign correspondent with postings in Jerusalem, Amman, Kabul, Islamabad, Tehran, and Abidjan.

Lyse is a Council Member of the International Council on Human Rights policy, an honorary patron of Canadian Crossroads International, and a member of Friends of Aschiana UK which supports working street children in Afghanistan.

caroline neil

Fail to prepare – prepare to fail

He assured me that his fixer/driver had it all in hand…

The journalist from a well-known and popular men's magazine regarded me with a mixture of disdain and surprise accompanied by an "oh dear, here we go again" attitude. We were in Goma, a small town in the eastern region of the Democratic Republic of Congo; a country plagued by war and tainted by an ongoing rebel problem, along with a lawlessness which meant that its citizens were raped one week by the army and the next by the rebels. And it wasn't just the women.

As a security advisor, I had suggested to him that for his trip up country into rebel-held areas he should take two vehicles, ensure that his fixer/driver had sufficient water, food and medical equipment for all members of the team, and be sure that the vehicles were road-worthy and carried a spare tyre with the correct equipment in the event of a breakdown. In addition to this, some form of water purification, as the water in the DRC would make you seriously unwell. Generally, this type of trip has to be planned to consider all eventualities. I had also suggested that he check in with the Pakistani UN media coordinator to get the latest information on the rebel and army movements. To all seasoned security consultants and journalists who report in and around war zones this is bread and butter common sense, but as I was soon to discover is not common practice if you had not done hostile environment (HE) training.

When things go wrong my job is to protect journalists and facilitate them chasing a story until the last possible safe moment, sometimes as the bullets are flying. Car crashes are the biggest killer of journalists and when someone has lost their leg as a result of a car accident they are lucky if we can get them to medical assistance, let alone back to their loved ones.

"Mr man's magazine" subsequently had a car accident up country, one hour from the nearest UN base. The driver was driving too fast, hit a pot hole on the dirt track and rolled the car, which ended up immobilised with either the rebels or the army firing off in the distance. His driver was badly concussed, his camerawoman badly shaken up and not one of them had a medical pack. The camerawoman left the country two days later and the sheepish journalist crawled back to Goma, having been evacuated by the Indian Army. I often wonder what happened to the driver.

Opposite page: A FDLR rebel fighter watches over civilians ordered to destroy a bridge at the village of Peti in eastern Congo. ©REUTERS/Finbarr O'Reilly

"Mr man's magazine" could hardly look me in the eye as he recounted his tale in a bar in Goma. He refused to give me any of the pictures he took of the smashed up vehicle, so I could use it for training, and he avoided me at the airport some days later. You can make your own assumptions as to why that would be!

From my own experience, waking up at 5 am and going to check the security of my hotel in northern Iraq was an eye opener. There were only rooms on the ground floor and they did not lock. To find that the guards were all asleep in the gatehouse with their AK-47 rifles propped against a plastic chair was a wake up call, and the following night I moved to a more secure (and expensive) hotel down the road. Sometimes safety is more important.

And in the days when it was "cool" to drive like a Formula 1 driver, having a blowout at 80 mph in an armoured vehicle driving between Basra and Baghdad was somehow not so "cool". I'd been constantly telling the driver to slow down but he didn't listen. Thankfully, we found a spare wheel and kit in the boot. You can imagine me standing on the side of the highway with a bunch of journalists all wearing flak jackets, trying to blend in with the desert – it would have been funny had it not been so dangerous.

An hour is a long time in Iraq, but my team reckoned we had about 20 minutes before the "bad guys" found out our location and started amassing a team to kill us. The driver actually responded well under my supervision while changing the tyre, but I am sure it didn't do much for his testosterone-fuelled ego. Guess who organised the packing the next time we went on a road trip?

Danger perception is relative, and I have seen different people's risk perception range from the sublime to the ridiculous: the ludicrously "elf and safety" who won't step out of the hotel, to the downright dangerous to be around "hack", trying to prove him or herself to their peer group and wishing for a chest big enough on which to pin medals. Yes, I've taken some premeditated risks, and have encountered some tricky situations, but I always thought about possible repercussions, had the right equipment and training and had the common sense to have left a plan with someone, in case I didn't come back.

Journalists and ex-soldiers are privileged to be able to choose to live and work in conflict and post-conflict zones. Where normal people suffer daily hardship, poverty, death and illness, the lawlessness and disaster in these areas make the headlines and get prime

a note on hostile environment training

The old-school thinking back in the late 1990s, when we first started hostile environment training, was that soldiers, ex-soldiers and journalists were not natural bed partners. Journalists thought soldiers and ex-soldiers were trying to hamper their every turn and make their lives difficult. Soldiers and ex-soldiers thought journalists were reckless fools, who endangered others to get foolhardy stories and then expected someone else to get them out of the "shit".

I am pleased to report that now, HE training has gone some way to making both sides realise that they have much in common: they both live and work in the most dangerous areas around the globe. My job for the last 13 years has actually been to facilitate journalists getting that 'BAFTA' story, and ensuring they and the rest of the team comes back alive.

HE training has saved lives and has evolved from the early days, keeping journalists and their teams safe while making them more self-sufficient. How to get through checkpoints, getting the story in crowds, getting the story before, during and after being shot at, getting the story having planned it thoroughly and taking the right kit to survive the latest earthquake – all these things are covered during the training. The first aid training is 'get in and get dirty', hands on, and save lives – rather than some courses which teach you how to tie neat tidy knots on bandages. Trying to get people to carry first aid kits in the bottom of their bags is still an uphill struggle – but we're getting there.

time slots in the national news. The least we can all do is to be prepared, make sure we have plans in place and we know what we are doing. We should ensure we can deal with emergencies ourselves or if we have to ask for help, try not to burden the already over-stretched local system. I am rather hoping that "Mr man's magazine" has now learnt from his mistakes and at the very least has now attended one or more HE training courses. I wonder if he now still fails to prepare and therefore prepares to fail, when trying to get his headline story in a hostile region?

Caroline Neil *is a security and risk management consultant, working mainly in Africa, the Middle East and South America. She provides advice for a broad range of companies, from large and small media corporations to oil and construction multinationals.*

After spending ten years in the British Army and having worked all over the world, she put her experience to use as a freelance security consultant and has now worked with journalists in conflict areas for the last 13 years. She has worked as Head of the BBC High Risk safety and security team and was also responsible for a project to assist journalists who had post traumatic stress from working in conflict areas.

general safety advice for journalists

Before you go

- Research the place you are going to before you leave. Be aware of the language, culture and customs of where you are travelling to.

- Be clear about travel arrangements – for example, who you will meet, the address of the hotel, transport logistics and who your family should call if there is a problem back home.

- Leave the contact details of the people you are meeting with a trusted person.

- Make sure all your banking and personal administration is up to date, including your will.

- Ensure you have travel insurance to cover you to and within the country and surrounding countries in case of problems. Ensure you have life assurance if you are going to a hostile country and that it covers all your outgoings back home, in the event that your life assurance policies are invalidated by war.

- Ensure any insurance policies are covered for war and terrorism.

- If appropriate, carry ID on you and keep copies of important forms of ID (passport, vaccination booklet, traveller's cheques, medical card) somewhere safe – for example, on webmail, or carry photocopies if the country allows.

Clothing

- Respect the local dress code and err on the conservative side; no shorts for men, nor short sleeves for women.

- Consider that ponytails, necklaces or jewellery can be easily grabbed in crowds – you may want to tuck these in, or avoid wearing them.

- Shoulder bags can be easily snatched – consider wearing bags which can be worn across your body, or a rucksack (consider wearing it on your front in crowds).

- Consider wearing shoes that you can run in and that will protect your feet in debris – flip flops are not ideal, sturdy boots may be better.

- Make sure your body armour and helmet fit properly – not having properly-fitted or comfortable body armour means it might not be worn, and it will not provide proper protection when needed. Respirators/masks should also fit properly.

Transport

- Avoid unlicensed cars and taxis – using a reputable company is always preferable. Book taxis from the hotel or from the licensed offices at airports.

- Agree the cost of the journey before you leave even if the taxi has a meter.

- If alone, think about where you sit. Sitting behind the driver makes it difficult for him to touch you.

- Remember some taxis have automatic locking when the vehicle is moving.

- While using buses, sit near a driver or near a group of people. If in trouble, sound the bell continuously.

- Avoid empty carriages and make sure you don't arrive back at empty stations late at night in the dark.

- Keep your baggage and possessions within sight and reach of you at all times. Consider chaining your belongings to your chair in case you fall asleep.

Accommodation

- Know where you will be staying beforehand. Make sure you know where the hotel is located and Google its location. If travelling alone, choose a higher standard of hotel than you would if you were travelling with colleagues.

- Try to take a hotel room next or near to your colleagues.

- Don't get in to an elevator or walk in a corridor if you think somebody is following you.

- Don't open the door to strangers. Look through the keyhole to check who is knocking, if you can't see them don't open the door; call the reception desk or security.

- Lock all of the doors and windows when you are going out, even if it's only for a few minutes. Ensure the doors are locked when you are in the room.

- If the door lock does not have a chain, consider moving furniture in front of the door when you sleep, so there is a barricade – particularly if the door has an electronic lock, as these are easy to bypass.

- Avoid staying on the ground floor as your room will be easily accessible via the window or balcony.

- Think about using 'Pacsafe' – anti-theft travel gear – to secure your expensive belongings. Pacsafe [http://www.pacsafe.com]

Personal safety

- Be aware of how your contacts/sources see you. You may be dressed appropriately, but cultural misconceptions may make you appear promiscuous.

- Think about the type of conversations you strike up and consider how much eye contact you have with strangers – it can be misinterpreted as flirting.

- Hugging and smiling with other colleagues in some countries can be misinterpreted and raise the risk of unwanted attention.

- Think about whether you should drink alcohol alone with contacts/sources, and if you do, consider limiting it. Alcohol could encourage a source to make a pass, and drinking can slow your ability to respond. Be aware in some cultures that not drinking alcohol may also cause offence, so have a good reason if you do not wish to join in.

- Be careful of sharing details of your work with people you don't know – it might be better to say you work in a different profession, such as teaching; careless talk may compromise your story.

- Ensure your online profile does not compromise the work you are doing. Be careful what comments and pictures you post on Facebook for example.

- When working in and around crowds, ensure that somebody is covering your back; preferably working in pairs.

- Consider carrying a basic phone that nobody would want to steal – keep your smartphone switched off in your bag.

- Consider keeping the number of someone senior in the army or police stored in your phone. Keep useful local numbers in case of an emergency.

- Consider carrying a second small, switched-off phone with you, if appropriate. It can be used as a back-up for emergencies. If you do keep a second phone, make sure it also has all the important contact numbers programmed inside. A basic, unlocked phone and a local sim card is more appropriate than a smartphone.

- Support staff, such as translators, fixers and drivers, can monitor the overall security of the situation and flag up potential risks.

Harassment, attack and sexual assault

- Make it clear that you will not tolerate inappropriate touching or comments from support staff, colleagues and sources.

- Saying you are married or engaged can sometimes deter unwanted attention.

- If you are alone and being harassed, have a cover story prepared, such as 'I am waiting for my husband/wife/colleague to arrive', and try to join a group of people – preferably of mixed sex.

- If you suspect you are being followed, try to go to a busy place, like a hotel. If possible stop a policeman (in a country where this is safe) and inform him, or stop somebody and ask them for directions or the time. This will distract the follower and give you the opportunity to assess the situation.

- If you are arrested, try your best to stay with a colleague and avoid being separated.

- Consider carrying a personal attack whistle or rape alarm, and carry it in your hand rather than your bag for quick use. Ensure it can be carried on airlines. Do no carry pepper spray, as it is illegal on airlines and in some countries.

- Hairspray and deodorant can be carried legally and used as a deterrent in cases of attack.

- Try to break the momentum. Distract the attacker with an unrelated topic, or pointing out something around you.

- Say you are HIV positive, menstruating or pregnant – but remember this may encourage them if they are HIV positive, and most attackers will not care.

- If you are cornered, consider your options and if you decide on aggression, shout and fight with 100 per cent of your energy.

- Consider not struggling, if you think your attacker is HIV positive, because drawing blood can spread the infection. Know where to obtain anti-retrovirals (ARVs) in the event of rape by somebody with AIDS.

Stress and post-assignment stress

- When your assignment is finished do not bottle up emotional distress. Talk to somebody you trust about your experience. Free counselling is available after covering conflict situations at the following address or consider asking your commissioning organisation for assistance. Dart Center for Journalism and Trauma [http://dartcenter.org/]

N.B. the websites listed are useful resources but not endorsements

top tips from women in the field

SECURITY
Door wedges and door alarms keep intruders from entering your room
A small can of hairspray or deodorant can be used in self defence

CLOTHING
In Muslim countries, consider taking a headscarf that can double up as a shawl.
Consider taking a cap which may make you blend in with the men in your team.

Consider wearing flat, lace-up shoes, so you can run in them.

Dangly earrings and expensive jewellery can attract unwanted attention and be pulled. If you want to wear earrings, wear cheap studs.

Consider wearing a fake wedding ring – it may keep unwanted advances away.

Cargo pants are hardwearing and easy to wash – but think about buying them so they are loose; tight fitting trousers show all curves and this may be offensive in more conservative countries. Consider wearing a loose-fitting long shirt to cover hips and thighs.

Wearing a vest under a baggy blouse will cover your chest when you lean forward and soaks up sweat.

Cotton knickers will help prevent infection.

Panty liners can be invaluable, especially if you don't get a chance to do laundry often.

Consider wearing a baggy skirt for long journeys as you can squat and go to the toilet without exposing all.

HAIR AND MAKEUP
Tie your hair back – in some countries, men find long loose hair sexually alluring and might want to touch it. But also be aware that ponytails may be easier to grab.

Be aware that in some countries, wet hair can be mis-interpreted as a sexual signal.

If you have blonde hair, consider covering up with a cap or a scarf in countries where this is an oddity and people want to touch it, or consider short term wash-in dyes.

Excessive makeup can also attract unwanted attention.

HEALTH
Sanitary towels are not as efficient as tampons – they smell in hot countries and are difficult to dispose of.

Tampons with a plastic or cardboard applicator keep germs away from intimate areas. Take more than you think you need, as pressure and change in your environment can change cycles. If you don't use them you can give them as gifts to national staff, who can't get them as easily.

Nappy bags or fragrant sanitary bags are useful for the disposal of sanitary towels and tampons.

Use feminine wipes for intimate areas – wet wipes upset the PH balance and can cause infection.

Consider bringing a treatment for thrush – the heat, lack of sanitary arrangements and wearing trousers can cause infection even if you have never suffered before, ie. Canesten Cream [http://www.canesten.co.uk/]

Be aware of the possibility of contracting bacterial vaginosis (BV) and take precautions to ensure that PH levels are kept in balance. If BV occurs take metronidazole (Flagyl tablets) See Balance Activ [http://www.balanceactiv.com]

If you are prone to cystitis, heat and lack of water can cause infection. Consider bringing cystitis tablets.

Bring condoms or female condoms if you intend to engage in sexual activity.

Consider bringing the morning-after pill in case of rape if going to high-risk areas.

If you are prone to period pains, paracetamol (which doubles up as relief for headaches) and ibuprofen (which doubles up as an anti-inflammatory) can be taken three times a day after food.

Consider carrying a small tin of powder – this will prevent rubbing bras under arms in hot countries.

Stick deodorant lasts longer than aerosol.

Consider bringing a SheWee so you can go to the toilet in difficult places without removing your trousers. SheWee [http://www.shewee.com/]